Sakai OAE Deployment and Management

Max Whitney

O'REILLY®

Beijing · Cambridge · Farnham · Köln · Sebastopol · Tokyo

Sakai OAE Deployment and Management
by Max Whitney

Published by O'Reilly Media, Inc., 1005 Gravenstein Highway North, Sebastopol, CA 95472.

O'Reilly books may be purchased for educational, business, or sales promotional use. Online editions are also available for most titles (*http://my.safaribooksonline.com*). For more information, contact our corporate/institutional sales department: 800-998-9938 or *corporate@oreilly.com*.

Editors:	Shawn Wallace and Brian Jepson	**Cover Designer:**	Karen Montgomery
Production Editor:	Melanie Yarbrough	**Interior Designer:**	David Futato
		Illustrator:	Robert Romano

Revision History for the First Edition:

2012-06-01	First release
2012-06-14	Second release
2012-08-21	Third release

See *http://oreilly.com/catalog/errata.csp?isbn=9781449318765* for release details.

ISBN: 978-1-449-31876-5

[LSI]

1345566137

Table of Contents

Preface

A Note on Names

The original Sakai software descended from work by Indiana University, Massachusetts Institute of Technology, Stanford University, University of Michigan, uPortal, and the Open Knowledge Initiative. Lots of the original code came from University of Michigan's framework, known as CHEF, the CompreHensive collaborativE Framework. (Programmers do love to stretch their acronyms.) As the new shared infrastructure matured, a joke ran through the community that this was *Iron Chef*, a reference to the Japanese competitive cooking show. It seemed right on the surface: this collaboratively built framework was stronger, smarter, faster, and more international than any of the preceding single-institution systems. It also felt right as an observation of the community in development: programmers and academics coming together across varied institutional cultures interacting in some highly formalized ways to duke it out over which implementation choice was best. Who would win the challenge? An established programmer from a long-committed university or a smart upstart designer from a tiny consulting firm? The software was ultimately named for the "King of Iron Chefs," Hiroyuki Sakai, with hope that it would be the winningest of all education and collaboration frameworks.

After a couple of years, an effort to rewrite the backend services was undertaken. This started out as the kernel rewrite effort, morphed into the kernel rearchitecture effort, then got clear enough that it became two separate but aligned efforts called *kernel 1* and *kernel 2*. A major user interface redesign was undertaken at the same time, addressing both the user interaction and user experience layers. Because the production version was numbered in the 2s, work on the next generation of the frontend of Sakai became variously known as *Sakai 3* and *3akai* (pronounced *three-ak-EYE*). It got maddeningly confusing to talk about Sakai 2 on K1 as distinguished from 3akai-ux on K2. The kernel team resolved on *nakamura* as the name for the backend services. This name benefitted from referring both to an Iron Chef, Koumei Nakamura, and to the first Japanese national to scale K2, Shoji Nakamura. Let it never be said that Sakai programmers don't love the act of naming.

The name of the overarching product, of which nakamura forms one element in the framework, is the *Sakai Open Academic Environment* (OAE). This name primarily serves to distinguish it from the other Sakai product, the *Collaboration and Learning Environment* (CLE). While OAE started out conceptually as the next version of CLE it is now clear that both OAE and CLE will continue on as distinct products in development and maintenance for as long as schools and organizations find them valuable. The numeric distinction between them had become misleading.

In practice, both systems get rebranded as soon as they're deployed. Sakai instances around the world are known variously as Vula, Tusk, bSpace, and many other names, each of which is meaningful to the local community. Often it is only the technical staff that speak of CLE or OAE on a given campus. It is the branded, art-directed, living community of interaction that the students and teachers talk about.

Conventions Used in This Book

The following typographical conventions are used in this book:

Italic
> Indicates new terms, URLs, email addresses, filenames, and file extensions.

`Constant width`
> Used for program listings, as well as within paragraphs to refer to program elements such as variable or function names, databases, data types, environment variables, statements, and keywords.

`Constant width bold`
> Shows commands or other text that should be typed literally by the user.

`Constant width italic`
> Shows text that should be replaced with user-supplied values or by values determined by context.

 This icon signifies a tip, suggestion, or general note.

 This icon indicates a warning or caution.

Using Code Examples

This book is here to help you get your job done. In general, you may use the code in this book in your programs and documentation. You do not need to contact us for permission unless you're reproducing a significant portion of the code. For example, writing a program that uses several chunks of code from this book does not require permission. Selling or distributing a CD-ROM of examples from O'Reilly books does require permission. Answering a question by citing this book and quoting example code does not require permission. Incorporating a significant amount of example code from this book into your product's documentation does require permission.

We appreciate, but do not require, attribution. An attribution usually includes the title, author, publisher, and ISBN. For example: "*Sakai OAE Deployment and Management* by Max Whitney (O'Reilly). Copyright 2012 Max Whitney, 978-1-4493-1876-5."

If you feel your use of code examples falls outside fair use or the permission given above, feel free to contact us at *permissions@oreilly.com*.

Safari® Books Online

 Safari Books Online (*www.safaribooksonline.com*) is an on-demand digital library that delivers expert content in both book and video form from the world's leading authors in technology and business.

Technology professionals, software developers, web designers, and business and creative professionals use Safari Books Online as their primary resource for research, problem solving, learning, and certification training.

Safari Books Online offers a range of product mixes and pricing programs for organizations, government agencies, and individuals. Subscribers have access to thousands of books, training videos, and prepublication manuscripts in one fully searchable database from publishers like O'Reilly Media, Prentice Hall Professional, Addison-Wesley Professional, Microsoft Press, Sams, Que, Peachpit Press, Focal Press, Cisco Press, John Wiley & Sons, Syngress, Morgan Kaufmann, IBM Redbooks, Packt, Adobe Press, FT Press, Apress, Manning, New Riders, McGraw-Hill, Jones & Bartlett, Course Technology, and dozens more. For more information about Safari Books Online, please visit us online.

How to Contact Us

Please address comments and questions concerning this book to the publisher:

O'Reilly Media, Inc.
1005 Gravenstein Highway North
Sebastopol, CA 95472
800-998-9938 (in the United States or Canada)
707-829-0515 (international or local)
707-829-0104 (fax)

We have a web page for this book, where we list errata, examples, and any additional information. You can access this page at:

http://oreil.ly/sakai_OAE_deployment

To comment or ask technical questions about this book, send email to:

bookquestions@oreilly.com

For more information about our books, courses, conferences, and news, see our website at *http://www.oreilly.com*.

Find us on Facebook: *http://facebook.com/oreilly*

Follow us on Twitter: *http://twitter.com/oreillymedia*

Watch us on YouTube: *http://www.youtube.com/oreillymedia*

Content Updates

August 21, 2012

- Updated Figure 4-1 with "REST/JSON" label.
- Fixed a typo in Figure 7-6: pre.ecample.edu became pre.example.edu.
- Clarified wording on page 55, and fixed spacing.
- Fixed a confusing line break on page 96, keeping -O together on one line.

Acknowledgements

I received a tremendous amount of assistance in writing this book. It is a far better book because of it.

Without the dedication of the entire Sakai OAE Managed Project staff, there would be no software about which I could write. I would particularly like to thank Ian Boston, Nicolaas Matthijs, Zach Thomas, and Carl Hall for taking the time over the last few years to work through the fundamentals of OAE with me, long before we even knew it was OAE; Daniel Parry for his freely available guides to the Cambridge deployments on the 1.0 and 1.1 series of OAE; Bert Pareyn for help with the CSS field guide; Scot Hacker for the WalkTime widget and pointers on widget development; Mark Walsh for pulling a functioning Oracle 11 pom.xml out of his hat. Valuable examples and advice were provided by Lucy Appert, Sam Peck, Chris Tweney, Chris Roby, D. Stuart Freeman, Oszkar Nagy, Christian Vuerings, Ray Davis, Jonathan Cook, Erik Froese, Lance Speelmon, Eli Cochran, The Githens, John King, and Michelle Hall from the Sakai communtiy and by Andy Sears, Mark Reilly, James Bullen, Jeff Pasch, Madan Dorairaj, Mark Triggs, Payten Giles, and Zach Elliott at my home department. I am grateful to Mark Dukes and Dan Burner of All Saints Company for permission to use the image of Paul Erdos from the Dancing Saints icon at Saint Gregory of Nyssa Episcopal Church in San Francisco and to Ludovic Poitou at Forge Rock for encouragement in using the OpenDJ Directory for the authentication samples.

I would like to thank David Ackerman for his foresight in championing this project from early days at NYU, and our CITO Marilyn McMillan for leading us succesfully through many a tumultuous year.

My editors Brian Jepson and Shawn Wallace performed an amazing feat in turning this book out mere weeks after the OAE 1.2 release date. I am particularly grateful to Brian for seeing the value in Sakai OAE and taking on this project before we knew we'd have code. Much credit must go to Ian Dolphin, who was my original sounding board for the usefulness of this book. The manuscript was made more readable by the input of my reviewers: Zach Thomas, Noah Botimer, and Denise Hand. All errors are uniquely my own, as are all unintentional descents into my native tongue, Unix.

OAE is about enabling communities of learning. This book would not have come into existence without the constant conversation within my communities: I am grateful to Holly Hudson, Dustyn Roberts, Alexis Goldstein, Herb Hoover, Adam Mayer, Far McKon, Bill Ward, Raphael Abrams, Shelby Arnold, Matt Mets, Ranjit Bhatnagar, Guy Dickinson, and all the members and visitors to NYC Resistor who challenged my assumptions as I talked this book through on many a long day at our hackerspace; Stefan Lisowski, Hilary Mason, Rob Faludi, and Michael Dory provided valuable counterweights to my occasional single-mindedness; my teachers: Dennis Shasha, David Weber, Jim Valhouli, Lalith Munasinghe, Sunil Gulati, Jim Shapiro, Edmund Phelps, and particularly Mr. Charlie Deardorff and Mr. Rick Parris, who will always have the honorific with me. I am grateful to Jim Bruce, who was a key mover at MIT when I got my hands on my first mainframe account, and has honored me with his coaching these past few years. Tremendous thanks to my dearest friends Tom Igoe, Joseph Hobaica, Clive Thompson, Denise Hand, Morgan Noel, my mother Ginger Whitney, and my sisters Beth and Alicia Whitney.

This work is dedicated to our Greg Sewell, the friends of whom continue to change the world.

CHAPTER 1

Why Sakai?

Sakai Open Academic Environment is an open source collaboration software system supporting teaching and learning at higher education institutions around the world. It is free for anyone to download, install, configure, and use. Sakai OAE brings together teachers, researchers, and students online to talk, write, and share, with the aim of enhancing the educational endeavor everywhere for everyone.

Putting Course Materials Online

The usefulness of an online analog to in-classroom instruction is now well established. The 1990 idea Tim Berners-Lee proposed for solving a problem of knowledge transfer among scientist cycling in and out of the European Organization for Nuclear Research has become so ubiquitous, it's easy to forget it started somewhere. Almost as soon as Berners-Lee had a prototype of the World Wide Web working, the Fermilab Theoretical Physics Department was linking and sharing seminars on it. Individual instructors all over the world created their own web pages to support their research and teaching; pages of great effectiveness that were no more complicated than an HREF and a center tag could make them.

Twenty years later, a healthy majority of instructors use some kind of learning management system to support teaching and learning in the classroom, whether it is home-grown, open source, or proprietary. It can be as simple as posting the syllabus, and updating it as the term proceeds in order to reflect the pace of this particular semester's group of students, or it can be as complicated as weekly automated quizzes, drawn from a pool of hundreds of potential questions, graded entirely by the machinery in order to monitor the level of mastery and shape the instructor's ensuing lectures. The many tools and ancillary systems are well known now and used to great effect by instructors, from in-class clickers to web-based grade books, SCORM modules with adaptive release features, blog post assignments with required peer response.

What could be automated in the drudgery of the educational process, has been. The departmental photocopier lies largely quiet. Administrative assistants have been trimmed from the budget, and student workers are sent on ever more creative errands to earn their stipends. Much like word-processing software, the field of learning management software has matured, the market has saturated. It is a "solved problem," as computer scientists say.

Relying on old tools, Sakai OAE does something new. It does not lead with tools to automate the administrative tasks around learning. There is no grade book yet written. Assignment creation and receipt functionality is in development but it doesn't appear in the 1.2 version of OAE covered here. The heart of OAE is simple collaboration around the materials students study.

Collaboration

OAE is built for sharing. Every element of the system focuses back on the questions of engagement: who are students studying with? What's the newest material a researcher has shared? Who is watching it? Who is commenting on it? From the student's perspective the questions are yet more personal: what do I have to get done tonight? Who's figured out number five on this week's problem set? Is anyone around to meet up for a study group? Where is that brilliant anthropology reading from last year, which is exactly the source I would need for this term's business course, if I could only dig it out from all the things I read online last year?

Students spend years interacting: across classes, across departments, across instructors. They go abroad and return home. They spend days in part-time jobs and unpaid internships. OAE always ties them back to where they've been before. The university education builds one experience upon another, expanding students' understanding of the world, then bringing them back to campus to reflect, to look inside and see how it has changed their understanding of themselves. Every experience builds on the last, inflecting, enlarging their comprehension of specific skills, of bodies of knowledge, of themselves.

College, at its best, provides a framework for youngsters to become adults. A difficult task of identity formation takes place in the extraordinary years from age 17 to 22. Kids try on ideas and dispense with them just as fast. A hundred extracurricular clubs encourage passing commitments en route to discovering deep interests and pursuing them. She tries out psychology and cognitive science before realizing she wants to be an actor after all. He delves into nineteenth century Victorian mores before resolving on the more intelligible area of combinatorics.

In the fleeting window between youth and responsibility, students try on a million different selves. When they do this on the public Internet it becomes, all unwitting, a part of their permanent record. The impact is sufficiently real that Germany has legislated against considering information on social media sites like Facebook in employment decisions, and the United States is now considering similar rules. Where it may not be possible to draw a straight line between a moment of misspent youth and a lifetime of employment discrimination, there is a chilling effect of knowing everyone will know everything, in perpetuity. Do students get locked in to an identity they would otherwise shed because to be seen to flip-flop, to flim-flam, is too terrifying to their social selves?

A Protected Space

In this context, OAE is an ivory-towered social network. Here is a space where students can learn the risks and benefits of sharing themselves electronically, while not being permanently burdened by errors made in the process. Learning involves failure first. OAE can be a place to fail safely, a social network still inside the supportive structure of the university.

Everyone, even grandparents, are online socially. Connecting to Facebook or to Twitter, taking just a quick peek at Orkut, is both extraordinarily gratifying and wildly distracting. Old friends, left behind, are still there, fresh and eager to hang out. There too are parents, former teachers, ex-boyfriends, grandpa, that kid from the show you did in tenth grade. Public social networks provide bright easy access to current peers and present teachers, but they also bring forward everyone a student has ever known. What was meant as a quick check-in with a classmate before recitation swiftly veers off into an instant message marathon with the girl back home. Much like the campus quad or the student center, OAE provides the immediacy of a social network, but partitions it to permit students to focus on their current studies. Home will always be a click away, but when they want to turn their attention to their present schooling, OAE provides a wall to protect them. Distractions can be quieted while they focus on their work.

Faculty are accessible to their students in OAE without having to commingle their private and professional lives. Teaching is highly personal. To know where to prod a student is to know where they are, how they are, what motivates them, what is just on the edge of their current understanding. The intensity of that engagement can be exhausting to maintain at all times in all environments. Marking OAE as a designated place to be available to students, like posting office hours, presents an opportunity for the best engagement, balancing accessibility with boundaries. Public social networks can be where faculty visit with friends and far flung colleagues. OAE then is the online equivalent of campus—when you arrive there, you are present to teach and to learn.

The Open Source Orientation

OAE, the open academic environment, is an open source system issued under the Apache license, version 2.0. It has been built by a consortium of higher education institutions across the globe, under the auspices of the Sakai Foundation. None of the people working on building OAE know what it will be when it is done. Everyone reading this book will become a contributor. By asking questions, testing scenarios, by simply deploying the software, and seeing how your students use it, you will be changing the shape of the software to come.

In a direct way, this book will show you how to customize OAE. You'll get a tour of the skinning infrastructure, changing the look and feel of the system. You'll install a few sample widgets, expanding the functionality of OAE to suit your local needs. Widgets can be written by anyone. They can stay highly customized and very local, or they can be abstracted and contributed back to the OAE community of schools via the Widget Library. A widget can be a small static tool, greeting each person by name when they log in. It can be an institutionally important workflow such as a widget being built at NYU to seamlessly take in video content in OAE, pass it off to a separate video repository where it is compressed and encoded, and return a permanent link in the OAE environment, without ever distracting the person who is preoccupied with uploading film of their cat.

 Cats on the Internet are an area of valuable study, as evinced by Ethan Zuckerman's 2008 Cute Cat Theory presented at the O'Reilly Emerging Technology Conference.

The source code for OAE is public. If you find a bug, you can fix it. For people who have worked in open source before, this is not such exciting news, for those accustomed to proprietary vendor code it is a sea change. The code is managed on Github, with a team of core programmers committing changes on a daily basis. You can issue a pull request and know someone will look at it and give you feedback.

Running an open source system does not mean being out on your own. The Sakai community has a large number of commercial affiliates, ranging from cloud source service providers to custom development teams. Longtime service providers like Longsight, Unicon, rSmart, and Sungard Higher Education provide a deep technical bench for schools starting new with Sakai products. Aeroplane Software and Hallway Technologies have established practices extending and customizing OAE for particular situations. Wiley Higher Education, IBM, Oracle, and Blackboard all contribute to Sakai, demonstrating a belief in the value and viability of this open source academic environment.

The Sakai community of educators, programmers, and administrators provide a wealth of freely available insight. The mailing lists are active day and night. As an international community, it's always daytime somewhere, and programmers never sleep.

Sakai OAE is not a revolution in education technology. The groundbreaking innovations of the 1990s are now all familiar. Rather, OAE builds on two decades of web experience to reduce the complexity presented in an LMS. In repackaging familiar tools, it makes them into something else. The strict top-down hierarchy of the traditional LMS is shed. OAE is only just what it needs to be in order to serve its community of teachers, students, and scholars. It is a framework for sharing, collecting, and remembering. It is a system in which many voices can work on an idea, until it becomes a single shared concept. It can be a series of private islands, or a pangaea connecting everything. As Antoine de St. Exupery observed about airplane engineering—great design is "not when there is no longer anything to add, but when there is no longer anything to take away."

CHAPTER 2

Installing Sakai OAE

Sakai OAE provides installations ranging from a kick-the-tires demonstration system to a fully customizable and rebuildable set of source files. This chapter covers three installations models:

Web Start

The Java Web Start installation downloads Sakai OAE and everything needed to get it running in a demonstration format. Web Start is a good choice if this is your first encounter with Sakai OAE. Java Web Start is the absolute fastest way to get a look at OAE's features.

Binary Jar

The compiled Sakai OAE jar can be downloaded and run using Java on a Linux, Mac, or Windows system. The binary is a fully functional instance of OAE. To run a small pilot with a handful of users, this is a fast and simple method of getting started. The binary install includes the default look and feel and employs the Apache Derby database.

Customizable Build

When you're ready to start customizing and scaling OAE, build the frontend and backend code. The buildable code relies on maven, and on the `3akai-ux` and `naka mura` repositories for customization work. The 3akai-ux repository contains frontend code for customizing the look and feel of OAE. The nakamura repository has the backend code for integrating LDAP as an authentication system, and for setting up on other databases such as PostgreSQL and Oracle.

The Quickest Install: Web Start

To get started fastest, use the Java Web Start version of the software. Java Web Start lets you get a quick look at the system before installing the full application.

Use the browser of your choice to connect to *http://sakaiproject.org/oae-v12-release*.

In the "Downloads" section of the Sakai OAE page, there's a section titled "OAE 1.2.0 Web Start (one-click download/run for Demos)." Click the link there to connect to *http://source.sakaiproject.org/release/oae/1.2.0/webstart/sakaioae.jnlp*.

Depending on the configuration of your computer, you may be prompted to let Java run. The Java Web Start system ensures that OAE runs in the correct Java version and that it is segregated from other parts of your computer. The initial download will be quite quick, as it is just grabbing an XML file. Give your computer a minute to download and start the application up. You'll get a challenge once it's finished initializing, since the Java Web Start version of Sakai OAE carries a self-signed certificate. As this is a demonstration system, it's okay to click through the self-signed certificate warning.

The Web Start launcher includes a disclaimer that this version of the install is not meant for production. You won't be able to use the email functions or a handful of other functionality. Click the `Launch` button. Web Start notifies you that Nakamura has been started but it takes a little while to get running. You can close that message without impacting anything. Go ahead and twiddle your thumbs for a minute or two, or do a couple rows of knitting or sudoku.

Once Nakamura has started, the Launch screen changes to indicate that Nakamura is running, and the `Open Sakai OAE` button becomes enabled. Go ahead and click it to start OAE now.

Your web browser will open and connect to `http://localhost:8080`. (See Figure 2-1.)

You have achieved Sakai OAE. Congratulations! Head on over to Chapter 3.

When you're ready to shut the system down, come back to the Java Web Start window and click the `Exit` button. This will shut the system down. If you try refreshing the browser window, you'll get an *unable to connect* error, since now there's nothing to connect to. You can start the Java Web Start version again any time by executing the *sakaioae.jnlp* file.

Binary Install

Installing a regular small scale instance of Sakai OAE really isn't much harder than using the Java Web Start version.

Use the browser of your choice to connect to *http://sakaiproject.org/oae-v12-release*.

In the "Downloads" section of the Sakai OAE page, in the section titled "OAE 1.2.0 Binary," click the link to open the folder at *http://source.sakaiproject.org/release/oae/1.2.0/binary/*. Download the binary Java archive published there with the name *org.sakaiproject.nakamura.app-1.2.0.jar*. You can store the binary anywhere on disk and run it from that location. For convenience, drop it in a folder named *binary* in your own home directory (e.g. */users/username/binary*). Later on, when you build the code from scratch, you'll want to have a *source* directory to keep everything straight.

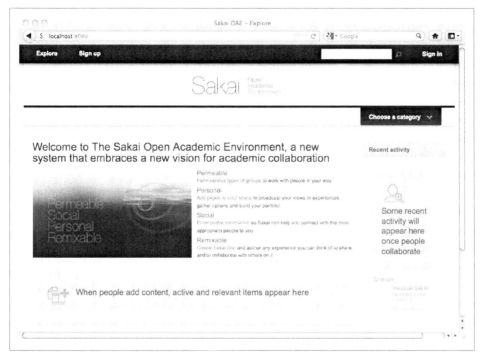

Figure 2-1. The Web Start OAE

If your preferred web browser is the command line, you can grab the OAE jar using curl. The curl browser is a great way to interface with the REST services OAE provides, making it the go-to tool for many OAE administrators. You can grab a copy of curl from *http://curl.haxx.se/* if it's not already on your system. (More information on curl is in Chapter 7.)

To download the Sakai OAE jar using curl:

```
curl -O \
http://source.sakaiproject.org/release/oae/1.2.0/binary/
org.sakaiproject.nakamura.app-1.2.0.jar
```

You can check that the file downloaded cleanly by comparing the md5 and sha1 checksums. For another layer of certainty, you can also check the GPG signature.

Install Java 1.6

Sakai OAE is built on Java. Test scripts and some subsystems are made available independently and rely on Python or Ruby, but for a basic binary installation, your only dependency is Java. Sakai OAE is certified on Java 6. You can see if Java is already installed and check the version at the command line:

```
java -version
```

If you receive something to the effect of the following output, then you are good to go:

```
java version "1.6.0_29"
Java(TM) SE Runtime Environment (build 1.6.0_29-b11-402-10M3527)
Java HotSpot(TM) 64-Bit Server VM (build 20.4-b02-402, mixed mode)
```

The first two digits of the version number are the relevant ones. "1.6" means you have version 6 installed and accessible. Java versions of 1.5 or (gasp) 1.4 need to be upgraded before you run the Sakai OAE binary. OAE hasn't been tested with 1.7 yet, so you may get some hiccups with a later version of Java than 6.

Each operating system will have its own foibles for getting to Java 6. Here's a thumbnail for some major OSs.

Ubuntu

To install Java 6 on Ubuntu, use *apt-get* at the command line:

```
sudo apt-get install openjdk-6-jdk
```

Note that you need to have sudo rights, or to have another way to become the root user, in order to install Java system-wide. If you don't have, or shouldn't reasonably get, root privileges then ask your system administrator to set up Java 1.6 for you.

Other flavors of *nix have their own package management strategies. Use the one you're most familiar with; apt-get has no particular strength over yum, apt4rpm, or any other package management tool.

Mac OS X

On a Macintosh, versions 10.5 and 10.6 are likely to have Java preinstalled. To get the latest version of 1.6, either run Software Update, or connect to *http://support.apple.com/downloads* and use the phrase "Java SE 6" with your operating system version number to find the correct update to download. If you've got more than one version installed, use the Java Preferences tool to make Java SE 6 the first version to try. If you prefer the command line, on 10.6 you can force the CurrentJDK to point to version 1.6:

```
cd /System/Library/Frameworks/JavaVM.framework/Versions
sudo ln -shfv 1.6 CurrentJDK
```

then check it again:

```
java -version
```

In version 10.7 and later, Java has to be installed from the Apple support site at *support.apple.com*. It no longer comes prebuilt with the operating system.

Windows

Oracle provides instructions for installing Java version 6 on Windows at *http://www.oracle.com/technetwork/java/javase/downloads*. Download and run the executable for your operating system (e.g., *jdk-6u32-windows-x64.exe* for 64-bit Windows). By default, the downloaded Java will install in the location *C:\Program Files\Java\jre6*. Check it at the command line with:

cd C:\Program Files\Java\jre6

.\bin\java -version

Be careful to distinguish this from the default version of Java for your system, which will remain the version returned by:

java -version

```
java version "1.7.0_01"
Java(TM) SE Runtime Environment (build 1.7.0_01-b08)
Java HotSpot(TM) 64-Bit Server VM (build 21.1-b02, mixed mode)
```

If you'd like to make version 6 the default for a command session, set your PATH to look to the Java 6 *bin* directory before any other:

set PATH=C:\Program Files\Java\jre6\bin;%PATH%

java -version

```
java version "1.6.0_32"
Java(TM) SE Runtime Environment (build 1.6.0_32-b05)
Java HotSpot(TM) 64-Bit Server VM (build 20.7-b02, mixed mode)
```

The PATH setting is specific to the current command executable, so exiting and starting a fresh command will revert to the default Java version.

Start the Binary Up

No time like the present to set up a minimal start script.

Create a new shell or batch script, depending on your operating system. Sakai OAE needs a bit more room than the reasonable defaults assumed by java. Specifically:

-Xms512m
 Start java with an initial memory allocation pool of 512 MB

-Xmx1024m
 Let the memory allocation pool grow up to 1024 MB if needed

-XX:MaxPermSize=256m
 Assign 256 MB for the permanent generation pool, where classes and associated metadata are stored

On Mac and Unix/Linux environments, create a file with the name *startup.sh* in the same directory as the *.jar* file:

```
#! /bin/sh
java -Xms512m -Xmx1024m -XX:MaxPermSize=256m -jar
org.sakaiproject.nakamura.app-1.2.0.jar 1> run.log 2>&1 &
SAKAI_PID=$!
if [ -f OAE.pid ]
```

```
then
    rm OAE.pid
fi
echo $SAKAI_PID > OAE.pid
```

The *nix style script captures the process ID and writes it to a file named *OAE.pid*, which the shutdown script will use later to identify which process to stop.

Make the start script executable:

```
chmod +x startup.sh
```

On Windows, create a file with the name *startup.bat* in the same directory as the *.jar* file:

```
@echo off

set PATH="C:\Program Files\Java\jre6\bin";%PATH%
java -Xms512m -Xmx1024m -XX:MaxPermSize=256m -jar
org.sakaiproject.nakamura.app-1.2.0.jar 1> run.log 2>&1 &
```

Windows doesn't use the process ID model of Unix. Instead, this startup script can be called by double-clicking on it. The OAE system can be stopped either by closing the command window, or by using Task Manager.

Start OAE with your spanking new start script by calling **./startup.sh** at the command line or by double-clicking *startup.bat*.

The console output will go to a file named **run.log** in the *binary* directory. On Mac and Unix/Linux platforms tail the run.log to watch the system start up. When you lose interest, you can cease to tail the log by clicking Control-C. That'll cancel your tail process and return you to the command line:

```
tail -f run.log
```

If you are running the system on an underpowered shared server or if your own little machine is really little, it may take a bit longer to start up. When you see the log entry ***INFO* [main] Startup completed** understand that is a programmer's truth, which is equivalent to a layman's barefaced lie. The statement that startup has completed means the startup script has finished what it considers to be its work: kicking off the start of the system. All those wiggly details about cacheing CSS and loading up the database for the first time have yet to finish. So, consider going to have a nice cup of tea and coming back in five minutes. Or turn to Chapter 1 and read it now. We know you skipped straight to the install chapter; it's okay! That was the right choice, because now you have something to go back and read while OAE initializes for the very first time:

```
*INFO* [main] Installing new launcher: jar:file:/Users/username/binary/
org.sakaiproject.nakamura.app-1.2.0.jar!/resources/
org.apache.sling.launchpad.base.jar, 2.3.0 (org.apache.sling.launchpad.base.jar.
1337036455648)
*INFO* [main] Loading launcher class org.apache.sling.launchpad.base.app.MainDelegate
from org.apache.sling.launchpad.base.jar.1337036455648
*INFO* [main] Starting launcher ...
*INFO* [main] HTTP server port: 8080
*INFO* [main] Startup completed
```

To find out when OAE is really done loading, watch the sling error log. Because one of the things Sakai OAE initializes on its first run *is* the sling directory structure, this may take a minute to come into existence. If you get the message `No such file or direc tory` give it a little breathing time and then try again.

For Unix style systems, you can tail the log as it runs:

```
tail -f sling/logs/error.log
```

When the sling error log stops throwing lines the system really is up and running. The ultimate line of the startup process is Felix's startlevel changed message:

```
*INFO* [FelixDispatchQueue] org.apache.felix.framework FrameworkEvent
STARTLEVEL CHANGED
```

Now connect your browser to *http://localhost:8080*. It will look the same as the Java Web Start version of the software, but it's a fully functional system now.

A Quick Domain Name Fix

At this juncture, attempting to connect to your machine under a proper domain name will be a bit underwhelming. Connecting to a fully qualified domain name will display the top bar of OAE and then stop rendering.

The Server Protection Service, discussed more thoroughly in Chapter 7, limits OAE's exposure to cross-site scripting attacks. Out of the box, it's configured explicitly for *localhost*. If you cannot, for whatever reason, access your OAE instance under the loopback network interface at *localhost:8080*, you'll have to take a quick dive into the innards of the OAE OSGi framework.

To hack up this quick fix, replace **yourdomain.edu** with the actual domain name for your system in the following steps:

1. In a web browser, open *http://yourdomain.edu:8080/system/console/configMgr*. When prompted, login with the username *admin* and the password *admin*.

2. Scroll down and click the component named `Sakai Nakamura :: Server Protec tion Service` to open its configuration panel.

3. For Trusted Hosts, replace:

   `localhost:8080 = http://localhost:8082`

   with:

   `yourdomain.edu:8080 = http://yourdomain.edu:8082`

   Click `Save`.

4. Quit and restart your browser application.

Now accessing *http://yourdomain.edu:8080* will properly display the landing page for OAE. You must quit and restart your browser because the admin credentials are cached in your browser. Once you log in as admin, you can't just log out.

It works! Of course, it looks just the same as the Web Start version, so this may not feel quite as exciting as you'd like. Rest assured that this is meaningfully different.

Shut the Binary Down

On *nix systems, for completeness, create another shell script—this one with the name *shutdown.sh* in the same directory where you created the *startup.sh* script. This script reads the process id from the file created by the *startup.sh* script and kills that process with extreme prejudice:

```
#! /bin/sh
if [ -f OAE.pid ]
then
  SAKAI_PID=`cat OAE.pid`
  kill -9 $SAKAI_PID
  rm OAE.pid
else
    echo \
    "No pid file found. Run 'ps -ef | grep nakamura' to identify the process to kill."
fi
```

Make the shutdown script executable:

```
chmod +x shutdown.sh
```

and shut OAE down:

```
./shutdown.sh
```

It doesn't hurt to do a quick process check after shutting down to make sure you have killed OAE:

```
ps -ef | grep nakamura
```

If all you get in response is the grep nakamura process itself, then you know OAE is shut down.

On Windows, use the Task Manager to shut down OAE. Right-click on the cmd.exe process associated with the *startup.bat* script and click End Task.

If you end up with multiple OAE instances running at some point, you'll get some confusing logging in the *sling/log/error.log* file. The first instance launched will have a hold on port 8080, so anything you do in a web browser will happen in the environment of that instance. If you unintentionally start up a second (or third, or fourth) instance of OAE, things will look normal on startup in the log associated with that instance, but when you click something in the web browser, you won't see any associated trail in the *error.log* file. If you're not getting the expected log entries, make a process check your first triage step.

Now you're ready to take a whirlwind tour in Chapter 3.

Building from Source

You may already be familiar with Sakai OAE, or have finished the whirlwind tour and are ready to customize OAE to suit your school or organization. You'll need the source code, the Maven build manager, and an installation of Java 1.6.

Be warned heading in to this section, that while it's one of the shortest sections, it may take the longest to complete. Depending on the speed of your network connection, and whether you already have a pile of useful stuff in your Maven repository, this build may take anywhere from 20 minutes to 5 hours. An hour is about standard for a stateside university on-campus connection. If you're working in an environment that meters your data usage, go someplace else for your first build. If you're planning to run this install over free city wireless in a beautiful pocket park, don't. Go get up close to an Ethernet cable. If your roommate is playing World of Warcraft, suggest she go check out the big room with the blue ceiling for a couple of hours.

The bulk of time and bandwidth in the initial build is used in retrieving artifacts for the Maven repository. Once you have them, builds will be relatively quick and extremely rare. Most of the work of customization is done live in the source files, or through configuration in the Sling OSGi web console. After the initial build, you'll do a major build again only when you're ready to redeploy a production jar tweaked to suit your school.

On *http://sakaiproject.org/oae-v12-release* in the section `OAE 1.2.0 Source`, there are four links to the four parts of the OAE system:

Frontend
> The 3akai-ux frontend code, including JavaScript, HTML, and CSS files. This is usually referred to as the sakai-ux code, and you'll rename it to that in the example code, but you may occasionally hear people say *three-akai* when talking about the frontend code (see the Preface).

Backend (Nakamura)
> The backend code. Much of the backend gets pulled down from other open source projects during the build process. Nakamura is Java code, built on the OSGi framework.

sparsemapcontent
> An open source sparse hash column oriented data storage layer. If you configure your system to use an Oracle database for storage, you'll need to bundle the Oracle drivers with sparsemapcontent.

solr
> Customized solr configuration for searching. Solr is bundled and configured with nakamura. The separate repository provides tools for setting up a stand alone solr server in a multinode architecture.

These subsystems were all tagged and tested together for the 1.2.0 release. The core elements, *nakamura* and *3akai-ux*, show the 1.2 tag. The supporting elements, *sparsemapcontent* and *solr*, are on a slightly different schedule, so they're tagged at 1.3.4 and 1.4.2 respectively.

The source code for Sakai OAE is managed by *git*, shared on github.com (*http://github .com/sakaiproject*). Later on, if you want to start contributing to the project, you can get set up with your own forks of the shared repositories. For now, download ZIP files of the code, so you can get started on basic customizations. For most of the customization covered in this book, you'll only need the *sakai-ux* and *nakamura* sources.

1. Create a directory, parallel to your *binary* directory, where the code will go. Call it *source*.

2. Connect to the link for the frontend code: https://github.com/sakaiproject/3akai-ux/tree/3akai-ux-1.2.0 (*https://github.com/sakaiproject/3akai-ux/tree/3akai-ux-1 .2.0*). This is the user interface code, and includes the files you'll need for skinning Sakai OAE to look like it belongs at your school. Click the ZIP button to get a copy of all the frontend code for this tag. Save it in your *source* directory.

3. Connect to the link for the backend nakamura code: https://github.com/sakai-project/nakamura/tree/nakamura-1.2.0 (*https://github.com/sakaiproject/naka mura/tree/nakamura-1.2.0*). This is the backend code, and includes the files you'll need for integrating and scaling Sakai OAE. Click the ZIP button to get a copy of all the backend code for this tag. Save it in your *source* directory.

The source code downloaded from Github is just one part of the whole which is OAE. The frontend source is 17 MB, and the backend just 7.5 MB. The bulk of backend source comes from other open source projects. Once built, the frontend code grows to 168 MB and the backend code consumes 280 MB.

You'll need one more piece, the *maven* build system. Sakai OAE 1.2 needs a minimum Maven version of 2.2.1. Check if you have it installed already and what version you're on:

mvn -version

```
Apache Maven 2.2.1 (r801777; 2009-08-06 15:16:01-0400)
```

If you don't have at least version 2.2.1, download it from *http://maven.apache.org/ download.html*. If you're on Ubuntu, you can do a quick:

apt-get install maven2

On Windows, be sure to set the environment and user variables as described on the Apache Maven download page. You'll also need Java version 1.6:

java -version

```
java version "1.6.0_31"
```

If you didn't get Java 1.6 set earlier in this chapter, pop back to "Install Java 1.6" on page 9.

1. Unzip the frontend and backend elements of the Sakai OAE source code.

2. On Mac and *nix use the unzip command:

   unzip sakaiproject-3akai-ux-3akai-ux-1.2.0-0-ga27a5b1.zip

   unzip sakaiproject-nakamura-nakamura-1.2.0-0-g33d7e98.zip

   On Windows, double-click the ZIP files to unzip them.

3. Move both directories over to more humane names.

   On Mac and *nix, use the mv command:

   mv sakaiproject-3akai-ux-e993f00 sakai-ux

   mv sakaiproject-nakamura-6407909 nakamura

   On Windows, do the same with the rename command:

   rename sakaiproject-3akai-ux-e993f00 sakai-ux

   rename sakaiproject-nakamura-6407909 nakamura

Change into the *sakai-ux* directory. In this location there is a *pom.xml* file which controls the Maven build for the frontend code. Maven looks to the pom in the working directory for its marching orders, so by calling Maven here you build the UX:

cd source/sakai-ux

mvn clean install

The UX code is largely self-contained. It relies on a handful of external systems, but all in all it's pretty concise. Building the UX takes under ten minutes on a nice high bandwidth pipe. The primary output artifact of the UX build is a jar called *org.sakaiproject.nakamura.uxloader-1.2.0.jar*. Once it's built this *.jar* gets dropped into your Maven repository, from whence the backend build collects it:

```
[INFO] Installing org/sakaiproject/nakamura/org.sakaiproject.nakamura.uxloader/
1.2.0/org.sakaiproject.nakamura.uxloader-1.2.0.jar
[INFO] Writing OBR metadata
[INFO] ------------------------------------------------------------------------
[INFO] Reactor Summary:
[INFO]
[INFO] Sakai 3 UX Loader Wrapper ......................... SUCCESS [1.051s]
[INFO] Sakai 3 UX File Hasher ............................ SUCCESS [4.780s]
[INFO] Sakai 3 UX Loader ................................. SUCCESS [38.168s]
[INFO] ------------------------------------------------------------------------
[INFO] BUILD SUCCESS
[INFO] ------------------------------------------------------------------------
[INFO] Total time: 45.027s
[INFO] Finished at: Wed May 23 22:06:23 EDT 2012
[INFO] Final Memory: 10M/161M
[INFO] ------------------------------------------------------------------------
```

To build the backend code, change into the *nakamura* directory and issue a build command from there. The backend is substantially larger, relying on signficant external frameworks to achieve its goals. Because of this, the memory allocated to Maven to do its work may need to be expanded before you build nakamura. This is done by setting the MAVEN_OPTS environment variable:

cd source/nakamura

export MAVEN_OPTS="-Xmx256m -XX:PermSize=256m"

mvn clean install

This'll take a while. Go get a coffee or a sparkling water. Or read some xkcd (say for example number 303 (*http://xkcd.com/303*)).

You're looking for a response like:

```
INFO] Sakai Nakamura :: Launchpad Standalone Java Application  SUCCESS [35.068s]
[INFO] ------------------------------------------------------------------------
[INFO] BUILD SUCCESS
[INFO] ------------------------------------------------------------------------
[INFO] Total time: 30:52.469s
[INFO] Finished at: Wed May 23 22:23:29 EDT 2012
[INFO] Final Memory: 55M/178M
[INFO] ------------------------------------------------------------------------
```

To Run as Root or Not?

Really, you don't want to run Sakai OAE as root. Why would you? Root can do *anything*. Even acknowledging that on a zone or a virtual machine the root user can be oddly restricted such that the impossible occurs and there's something root can't do, that's not an excuse to get sloppy. The easiest thing in the world to do is to let Sakai OAE run as root. You'll never run into permission problems, and you'll have access to *all the things*.

However, OAE will run with all the rights and privileges available on the whole box, and that may end up squeezing out other services. Like for example, login or ls.

The safest choice is to set up a sakai user just for running this software. Alternatively while you're sorting things out, run the system under your own userid. Then, when OAE bumps up against a permission or resource limitation, you'll know about it and can make an informed choice about how to increase resources or rights. Running as root means the first time you might hear of a problem is when the Sakai OAE installation takes your server down.

If up until now you've blithely been working through things while root, this is the moment to go straighten that all out. Make a sakai user, or commit to having your personal user id be sakai for a little while. Change the ownership of the source directory and its contents to the more limited user.

The source build comes with its own start script for Mac and *nix environments, so this time you don't have to create one. Call it from the *nakamura* directory with:

`./tools/run_production.sh &`

Take a look in the sling log to make sure it finishes starting up before you try to connect with a browser:

`tail -f sling/logs/error.log`

On Windows, there's a script as well this time, the `run_debug.bat` script in the tools directory. Somewhat unusually for Window, run this from the command line in the nakamura directory:

`.\tools\run_debug.bat`

OAE logs directly to the command session from the `run_debug` job.

Once you see:

```
org.apache.felix.framework FrameworkEvent STARTLEVEL CHANGED
```

open OAE up in your browser to make sure everything looks right before you start making changes:

http://localhost:8080

If the page looks like our beautiful and now familiar brand-spanking-new OAE, then you're good to go. See: short section—large chunk of your day.

CHAPTER 3

A Whirlwind Tour

OAE doesn't come with a user manual any more than Facebook, Google+, Orkut, or RenRen do. The user interface for the students, faculty, and researchers is designed to be straightforward after a bit of poking around. Local communities are left to develop their own customs without direction from the software creators.

This whirlwind tour exposes you to the key areas around profiles, courses, permissions, and content before sending you to the backend to customize them. If you'd prefer to click around and discover the system for yourself, by all means do so, then head to "Building from Source" on page 15 to start changing things up.

Choose Your Browser

OAE is designed to be browser agnostic, supporting as many browsers as possible, degrading gracefully when it runs in an unfamiliar browser. Testing targets the two most recent versions of Mozilla Firefox, Microsoft Internet Explorer, Google Chrome and Apple Safari at the time of a release. For OAE 1.2, released on April 25, 2012, this means:

- Mozilla Firefox 11 and 12
- Microsoft Internet Explorer 8 and 9
- Google Chrome 17 and 18
- Apple Safari 4 and 5

Create Your First Account

Whether you're working with the Web Start version, downloaded the binary, or decided to get down with Maven builds before looking around, let's get you in the system now.

You'll see a link at the top of your browser to Sign Up. This takes you to *http://localhost:8080/register* where you can set up your account (see Figure 3-1). The demonstration text is a tribute to Hiroyuki Sakai, the greatest of the great Iron Chefs. We'll assume you know how to enter (or make up) your name, email address, preferred username, and password. If you enter a username that's already taken, you'll see a little red *x* appear in the text entry field. As user number one, the only names you can conflict with are the demonstration username `hiroyuki` or the administrative account `admin`.

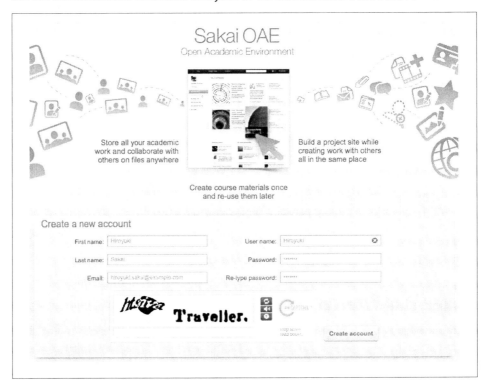

Figure 3-1. The sign up screen

Account creation integrates the reCAPTCHA system from Carnegie Mellon, now run by Google, to reduce the likelihood that spambots will invade your system. A captcha is a Completely Automated Public Turing Test To Tell Computers and Humans Apart. Technically it's a *reverse* Turing test, as the test asks you to convince a computer that you are a human, whereas the original Turing test asked a computer to convince a human that it also was human. Humans are, as of this writing, far more adept at detecting words in images than computers are, so many captchas rely on this difference in ability to sort people from bots.

A core technical principle of OAE is that wherever possible OAE will adopt well written open systems instead of rolling its own. Inclusion of reCAPTCHA embodies that principle while simultaneously helping to transcribe old books and newspapers. If it turns out that you are no better than a computer at discerning the words displayed, use the reload button (the two arrows in a circle) to ask for another.

Once you've created your account, OAE will automatically log you in and take you to your default dashboard.

The reCAPTCHA system relies on a web service running at Google. If you're setting up Sakai OAE off network, or have a highly restricted firewall sysystem, the interactive version of user creation will fail as it tries to connect to *recaptcha.net*. If you are fully offline, the registration page at *http://localhost:8080/register* will halt without an indication in the error log of what has failed, though you may see your browser attempting to contact *recaptcha.net* or *google.com*. If your network connection passes through a highly restricted firewall, the registration page will load in your browser but there will be no reCAPTCHA challenge at the bottom of the screen. In this case, clicking the `Create account` button will reload the page without actually creating the account.

Create Your Profile

Let's start with you who are.

Your personal profile is accessed by clicking on `My profile` in the lefthand navigation panel on the dashboard screen, or by selecting `My profile` from the drop-down menu accessible from the word `You` on the top navigation. By default, there are three sections to every person's profile: `Basic information`, `About me`, and `Publications`.

The `Basic information` section shows the information you added when creating your account: `First name`, `Last name`, and `Email`. People can also provide a `Preferred name` in addition to their formal first name. For roster and grading purposes, a school may need to populate and maintain the official name values for each profile. The preferred name allows each person to indicate what they will answer to, and allow that to be easily tracked against the official names by their instructors. The `Role/position` list defaults to an interesting amalgamation of university roles in English speaking countries, including the States, the UK, Australia, and South Africa.

The role `Faculty` got dropped from the default list; it was confusing permission conversations due to the differing meaning of the word in two of the contributing countries: in the U.S. a faculty member is a teacher and researcher; in South Africa the faculty is an area of study or a college. No worries though, you'll be able to change the default listing when you're ready to customize. See "Changing Drop-Down Menus" on page 53.

Tags and categories in the `Profile` can be edited in two ways: from the `List cate gories` pop up selection screen, or by typing directly in the text entry area. The categories listed by default are drawn from departments and areas of study common in the

Sakai community institutions. It is by no means exhaustive, and like the `Role/posi tion` values can be updated to reflect your institution's departments.

Direct text entry in the tags section gets at the more interesting case, what Thomas Vander Wal captured as "folksonomies" back in 2004. No system configurator or committee of configurators will think of the magic word that best describes you to your new community. If they could, next term the first year students will certainly reject it as overused and insufficiently unique. Free text entry allows people to tag their profiles with the specific ideas and descriptors they want people to know them by. If a tag closely resembles one of the prepopulated categories, that category will be suggested as you type. Let's go with something certainly not in the default category list: the world destroying villain of *Dr. Who*: "daleck." (See Figure 3-2.)

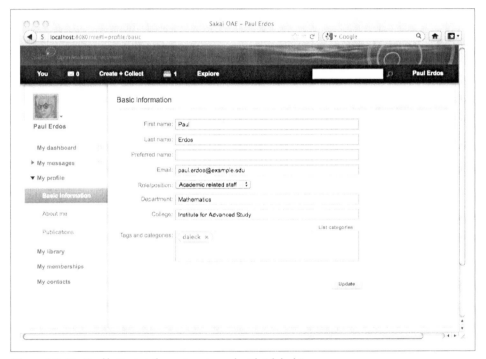

Figure 3-2. My Profile Basic information, tagged with "daleck"

The `About me` section is the essay section of the personal profile. The material you enter here is intended to be digested by readers rather than indexed by OAE. There's no formal limit on how much text you can enter. The text entry boxes are kept small to encourage conciseness.

To make yourself easily findable based on one of your interests or hobbies, it's best to enter it on that first `Basic information` screen as a tag rather than, or in addition to, the `About me` essays.

The final profile section Publications is the most formal, and the one most indicative of OAE's core academic mission. Basic bibliographic fields are assumed in the out-of-the-box install of Sakai OAE, but these can be updated to reflect your institution's established standards.

Last, add a photo to your profile. Chances are your first year students will do this before they do anything else. To upload an initial photo, click on the silhouette image over your name in the upper-left of the dashboard view, then select Change picture. You'll need to use an image that is stored locally on your computer, in JPG or PNG format. OAE is not yet configured to pull images from web sources or avatar hosting services. The image you start with need not be square nor any particular size. The crop and preview tool allows you to trim it before displaying it in your profile. To change the size of the trimmed image, click and drag a corner or edge of the highlighted area. To start over with a fresh selection box, click on the image anywhere outside the selection. The image will return to its normal coloration. When you're happy (or at least have reached a minimum of disatisfaction) with your profile image, click the Save new selection button. The picture over your name will update to display your new profile image (see Figure 3-2).

Now that you've shared some information about yourself, create your first site.

Create a Course and a Research Project

People learn in different ways. Some are autodidacts, absorbing material they encounter with minimal exchange with other learners or with instructors. Some are social learners, engaging the material by engaging with others. Any given person might be both an autodidact and a social learner depending on the topic, or on their level of mastery. Hans needs lots of conversation with experienced programmers to grasp the trade-offs among sort algorithms. Gretel needs a quiet room and a pile of problem sets to get a handle on partial derivatives.

Sakai allows you to tailor your project to accommodate different approaches to learning. Here we'll take a quick look at creating sites to support models at each end of that spectrum.

Lecture Course Online Companion

From the Create & Collect drop down menu at the top of the browser window, choose Create a course. Choose the Mathematics course template by clicking the associated Use this template button. This template is provided with Sakai OAE as an example of one way to structure a traditional lecture course. Enter a title for the course, say, **Partial Derivatives for Dunces**. The suggested URL is set to the course title once spaces and special characters are swapped out with something more URL-friendly. If you enter a course title that matches a URL already in the system, OAE will let you know and you can enter an alternative.

The URL stays the same through the life of the course in Sakai OAE. You can pop it in an email, on Twitter, or jot it on a napkin and know that students will be able to find the site consistently.

The description you enter here displays whenever someone browses a listing of courses in OAE. You can assign a tag or a category (or many of both) to the course, just the way you did to your profile. The same tags and categories are used in both places, so if you tagged yourself a *daleck* on the profile page, you can tag your course the same here. The partial derivatives course is a prerequisite for the pre-med program, so assign it the category `Medicine and Dentistry→Pre-clinical Medicine`.

There are three levels of publicity you can give to your new course site. You can make the course's existence completely public; this is, unsurprisingly, the `public` setting. Anyone who can get to your installation of Sakai can find out the course exists. They won't necessarily be able to see what is in the course; that is controlled by the membership settings. Another option is to make the course visible only to people who have accounts and have authenticated to Sakai, the `Logged in users` setting. This is akin to putting up a poster in your college's student center or inside the library building. Only members of your community can see information about it. The third option is to make the course invisible to anyone who isn't a member of the course. This one—the `participants only` setting—is the sharing equivalent of "ain't nobody's business but my own." You might want to keep your course invisible if it's a proposed course that may not make it past the curriculum board this semester or if you have an over-eager student body who will deluge you with requests for access as soon as they know you're teaching remedial calculus. Which brings us to the last setting: membership.

Sakai OAE supports three models of enrollment management by default: totally casual, totally controlled, and upon approval. The setting `People can join automatically` lets anyone with an account join the course at will. If they're interested, they can just join, and if they get bored they can just as easily remove themselves. The setting `Managers add people` allows you to have complete control over who joins.

The middle ground is the `People request to join` setting. Potential students can click a button to pass you a request for membership in the course. You then approve it before they gain access to the material in the course. This can give you a handshake moment, when you can ask potential pupils about their interests and background in advance of them turning up for the first lecture. For now, set the course to be discoverable by the public, and let people join automatically. (See Figure 3-3.)

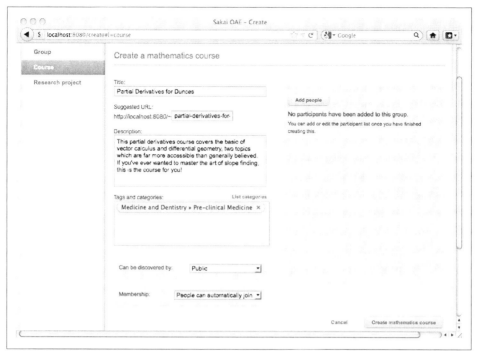

Figure 3-3. Creating a new course

It's entirely possible to create some unusual permission combinations. For example, say you make your course discoverable only by participants, then decide that people can join your course automatically. Try not to be hurt if no one signs up; they can't see it to join it. If you make your course public and set the membership to be controlled only by the course managers, and you happen to be a Booker Prize winner teaching a small writing seminar, expect students to deluge you with emails or even phone your office telephone line trying to get in to the course. If you go the totally public and tightly controlled route, put a note in your course description about how learners can express their interest so you don't end up with a crowd camping outside your office.

Click the `Create mathematics course` button on the lower right. It takes a few seconds for the system to copy over all the elements of the mathematics template. When it's done, your browser refreshes with the landing page of the course site. Take a look at the URL in the browser window. It consists of just three parts: the domain name for your OAE system, a tilde (~), and the URL-safe version of the name of your course site. If you later change the name of your site, the URL will remain the same as it is now. To see this, update the course site settings, as shown in Figure 3-4.

Figure 3-4. Accessing the course settings menu

To the right of the `Message` button is the group configuration drop-down menu, indicated by a gear icon (see Figure 3-4). Select `Settings` from the gear menu and change the title to `Partial Derivatives for Dreamers`. Click `Apply settings` and you'll see the title of the course change to this much more attractive version. The secret frustrations of the topic will persist in the address bar of your browser (see Figure 3-5). The only way to change that URL is to create a new course.

Figure 3-5. The URL remains the same even if a course title changes

Let's create a student now, so you can see the site from the learner's perspective. Before you go away and diminish your privileges, take a click around the lefthand navigation. There's the material you would expect to see: `Syllabus`, `Lectures`, `Problem Sets`, and `Participants`. There's also some you might not expect in an old fashioned learning management system: `Course website`, `Organization Notes`, `Lecture Template`, and `Library`.

Open the management menu for `Organization Notes` by clicking the downward pointing arrow that appears when your mouse is on that item and selecting `Permissions` (see Figure 3-6). Notice that the `Organization Notes` page, which is about the internal policies for this class, is viewable only by the lecturer and the teaching assistants (see Figure 3-7). Students don't see it at all. The teaching assistants can't edit it. T.A.s are consumers, not producers of guidelines in this particular class. (You're an autocrat of a lecturer, aren't you?)

Log out and make yourself another account, the same way you made your first one. Once you're logged in as your new self, enter **derivatives** in the search box at the top

Figure 3-6. Accessing the management menu for Organization Notes

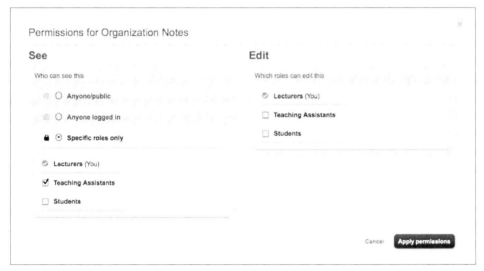

Figure 3-7. Permissions dialog box for the Organization Notes section

of your browser window. Sakai OAE will suggest the *Partial Derivatives* course as soon as it recognizes what you want, or you can click on the magnifying glass icon to kick off the search. If you had set the Partial Derivatives course to discoverable only by participants, you wouldn't be able to find it via search now. Once you've found it, access the course site by clicking on the course name. As a visitor there's less visible than when you were logged in as the instructor; just the `Syllabus` and `Course website` sections appear (see Figure 3-8).

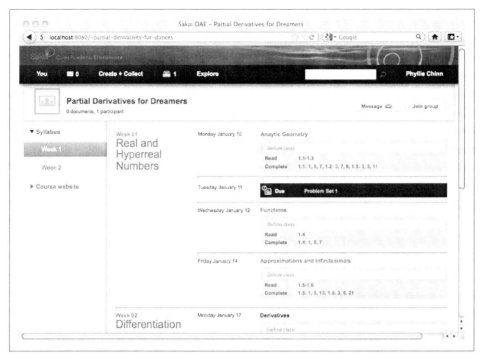

Figure 3-8. How the Partial Derivatives course looks to a window shopper

Along the top bar with the title of the course you'll see a button to send a message to the group, and a button for joining up. Click the Join group button and then refresh your browser. Now you have access to all the student materials for the course: the lectures, problem sets, library, and list of participants. You still can't see the material intended just for the lecturer and teaching assistants, nor can you access the drop down menus which control the left hand navigation elements or the group configuration gear menu.

Easy communication is one of the guiding principles of OAE development. Whether or not you're a member of the course you can send a message to everyone in the class. Click the message button. The to field is filled in with the name of the course site. Write a note and send it off. Everyone who is a participant in the course at the time you send your message will get a copy, including yourself.

The envelope icon at the top of your browser updates to show you have 1 unread message in your inbox. Click on the envelope to see a preview of the new message. Click the Read full message button to go to your inbox. Notice that the to line shows the name of the course. From the inbox view, you can mark messages read or just delete them (see Figure 3-9).

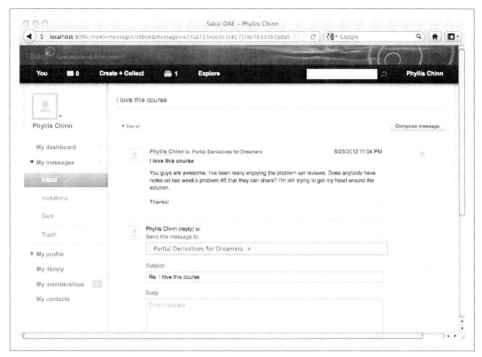

Figure 3-9. Exchanging messages within Sakai OAE

Course site templates focus on the interactions of students with their instructors, teaching assistants and with each other. Research project templates take a more constructivist approach, focusing on the individual learner.

Research Project

To create a research project, select `Create a research project` from the `Create + Collect` menu. Select `Use this template` for the simple `Research project`. Let's say this is a research project to go along with the Partial Derivatives course. Name it **Calculus on the Web** and set it to the most restrictive sharing settings: discoverable only by participants, with membership set to `Managers add people`. Don't add any participants, as this is a private research project (see Figure 3-10). Click the `Create research project` button. Like the course site, you'll be delivered to the landing page for your new research project once it's created.

Next, on the Introduction page, click the `Edit page` button. To exercise the revisions feature, replace the template text with some thoughtful summary information about this research into Calculus on the Web. Click **Save**, then make a few more changes and click the **Save** button again. Now take a look at the history of edits by clicking the `Page revisions` button (see Figure 3-11). Every save of your document appears as an entry

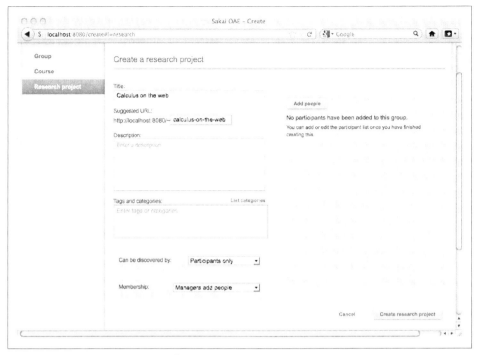

Figure 3-10. Creating a new research project

on the revision timeline, stamped with the time and author. You can view an earlier revision by clicking on the time and date of the entry. If you decide you want to throw some work away or, more likely, restore an earlier draft after accidentally deleting material, click the `Restore` button for that draft. That version becomes a new entry in the timeline, with the current time and date. Be a little careful where you click in the `Revisions` timeline; it can be dangerously easy to restore an earlier draft. While you can always restore over a restoration, it does eventually feel a bit like untangling twine the kitten's been at.

Before leaving this research project, take a quick look at adding content. Click `Library` on the lefthand navigation of the Calculus on the Web project. The Library displays a message that you don't have any content in the project's library yet, as well as a suggestion to `Add content`. Click that link to start creating and linking in materials. First, add a link to a website, say the Khan Academy calculus resources: click `Add link` on the lefthand navigation. For the link, enter *http://www.khanacademy.org/#calculus* and pop something in the `Title` field such as "Khan Academy's awesome calculus section". Click the `Add` button in the middle of the window. The Khan Academy link appears in the `Collected Items` section. There's a drop-down menu listing the libraries you can save this item to; it includes your private library, the *Partial Derivatives* course, and this *Calculus on the Web* research project. The selection defaults to the group from

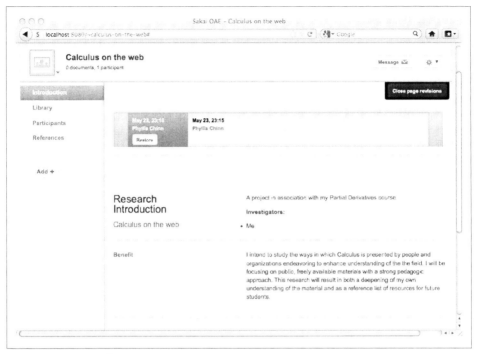

Figure 3-11. A pair of page revisions

which you started: *Calculus on the Web*. For the purposes of this example, change it to `My library`.

Take a look at the permissions here, which differ significantly from the permissions available to be set on groups and on pages within a group. Under `Khan Academy's awe some calculus section`, click `Add permissions`. There are three options for who can see this content: `Public`, `Logged in users`, and `Only me`. When you are adding an item to a collection there is no option to limit the visibility to a set of participants. Visibility is set when you include the item to a course or a research project. Let's make this link visible to the public.

The Copyright section is vitally important in the academic environment. Much of the material used in teaching is the result of the hard work of professionals. Copyright protects the intellectual property rights of these workers. Addressing copyright status in OAE opens the conversation with students about how to use others' work responsibly.

The OAE system identifies every element added to a collection with the copyright state of the item. The Khan Academy educational content is provided under the Creative Commons Attribution Noncommercial ShareAlike license, so select the `Creative Com mons` option from the `Copyright` menu. Click `Save` then click the `Done, add collected` button.

Because the link was added to your library, not to the research project's library, you'll be returned to Calculus on the Web's library with the note that your library is indeed still empty. Click `Add content` again, and we'll look at adding existing content to the project. Select `All content` from under `Use existing content`. You'll see absolutely everything you have access to in the system, including the student accessible materials from the *Partial Derivatives* course site. There's not a whole lot there yet. Check the checkbox next to `Khan Academy's awesome calculus section` and click the `Add` button at the bottom of the list of materials. This time the link appears in the `Collected items` section, but doesn't have the options to edit the item or to add permissions. The descriptive data for an item is only set one time, when you upload it. The item inherits those details every where it goes. Double-check that you are saving this collection to the *Calculus on the Web* library then click `Done, add collected`. At long last, you've got something in your research project library.

Click the title *Khan Academy's awesome calculus section* and you'll be brought to the item's profile page (content gets a profile just like people do) (see Figure 3-12). Along the top there's information about the visibility of the link as well as where it's being used and by whom. Below the preview of the link's content, there's descriptive information about the link, including when it was added to OAE and what copyright is associated with it.

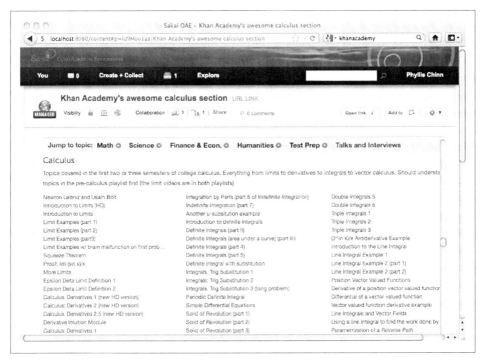

Figure 3-12. Content gets a profile, just like people do

Most folks in OAE will spend all of their time in course sites and working on projects, either alone, in clubs, or with their cohort. For us, this is just a whirlwind look at sites before digging into the backend of the system.

A Quick Trick for Checking Permissions

Sakai OAE keeps track of you while you're logged in using a cookie named `sakai-trusted-authn`. Regardless of how many tabs you open in a browser, you'll be logged in to OAE. This is terrific if you want to compare your work in a current class with the version you taught last semester. Just bring the two sites up in separate windows on your cinema display.

It's lousy for testing out permissions, however. When you want to check on how a course site appears to a test user or to an anonymous member of the Internet public, the constantly logging out and logging back in is a giant distraction. To reduce the virtual doorway effect, use a second browser like Firefox. If you're a devotee of Firefox, then use your operating system's default browser, whether Internet Explorer or Safari. It won't hurt this once to use it for testing. Cookies aren't shared between browser products, so you can maintain two live connections to OAE at the same time. To reduce confusion when checking permission settings, do something to differentiate the look of your two browsers: for example hide all the top bars on the browser of your less powerful user or use Firefox's full screen view for your more powerful user.

Changing the Dashboard

When you first log in to Sakai OAE you start out on your dashboard screen. Much as the name implies, this is the overview of what's going on in OAE right now (see Figure 3-13). On the lefthand navigation, you can rearrange the items according to your own priorities, with some exceptions: the My dashboard and My messages sections can be swapped, but will always remain the top two items in the left navigation. If you put My dashboard at the top, when you log in to OAE, you'll automatically get the dashboard view. If you put My messages at the top, you'll land in your inbox when you first log in. The items for my contacts, library, profile, and membership can be arranged in any order, providing they remain below dashboard and messages. To rearrange the left navigation items, click on the item title and drag it to its new position. You can rearrange subsections as well. Different people will have different preferences. The best set up may change through the course of the semester, and depending whether you're focusing on coursework or research.

The You drop-down menu on the top navigation will remain in the default order no matter how you arrange your left navigation. This achieves a balance between customization and support. The lefthand navigation is owned by the user, while the drop-down menu is guaranteed to stay exactly the same, so support staff can predictably offer instructions.

The top part of the main section cycles through content, groups, and contacts that you might find interesting. The algorithm for what gets displayed to each person is pseudo-random. Nonetheless, it implements the idea of serendipity. By way of example, my writer friend Clive follows almost 500 people on Twitter, some of them quite loquacious. He's experimented with prioritization algorithms, but ultimately it turns out any selection of those, given true attention, is better than trying to skim all of them. He's set up a client that draws his attention, almost randomly, to just a handful everyday. Since he's already done a lot of vetting for quality in who he follows, the results tend to be really interesting. The paradox of choice is defanged. Random's not such a bad prioritization scheme after all.

Figure 3-13. The default dashboard

If you find the carousel effect distracting, click on any of the three dots under the suggestions. The display slides to a single set of suggestions then stays there.

Below the suggestions, three sections highlight your recent activity: content you've added, groups you've joined and contacts you've established. This section is subject to the most customization. The areas here are called *widgets* and they're programmable chunks of Sakai OAE you'll hear more about in Chapter 6. Click the `Add widget` button at the top right of the window to see a list of the available widgets installed out-of-the-box (see Figure 3-14). As you click the `Add` and `Remove` buttons, the dashboard will update in the background, giving you a preview of your new dashboard. Click the

Add button next to the Most popular tags widget, then click the little x to close the widget screen. This widget displays the most used tags through the system. Clicking on a tag opens the search view, with all the results for that tag. At this moment the results aren't all that interesting, but as material is added to OAE interesting patterns emerge.

Figure 3-14. Adding a new widget to the dashboard

Finally, you can move your widgets around on the lower part of the main section. Click on the widget's title and drag it to its new position. Like My dashboard and My mes sages, the Suggested area always stays at the top of this section.

To reduce the number of widget columns from the default of three, click the Edit Layout button.

The Public Face of Sakai

The university is not just about what happens inside the ivory tower. How education engages the experience outside its walls is more important every day.

Many universities have a highly curated public web presence. These are quite good at serving the interests of potential students, of faculty and staff in their capacity as employees, and of students needing to navigate internal policies. Getting work in progress through an onerous approval process though can keep it locked up on an individual's web page. If a web page hasn't been redesigned since it was created in 1992—let alone been tuned for modern SEO—then it might as well be posted on the hallway bulletin board.

To get a sense of the public experience of the OAE, log out of the system. You're returned to the same page you saw when you first installed OAE, but now it will look a little different. On the right side, there's new information in the recent activity section. Because the link to the Khan Academy was marked public when it was added, it will pop up in this area. The research project *Calculus on the Web* won't show up, as it was set to the most restrictive privacy level.

Scroll down to see the Featured Content section. Along with the Khan Academy link, the public course website of the *Partial Derivatives* course you created appears here. Any course section or content item that's marked public is a candidate for display on the home page of OAE.

OAE can also be browsed by category. Click the Choose a category link to expand the category scroller (see Figure 3-15). These categories are the same ones you used in creating your profile, creating a course or project, and adding content. By adding a category to your materials in OAE, you, in effect, publish it (but only if you also mark it public). By contrast, tags don't bubble up to the public view of OAE. As folksonomy, they stay local to the community.

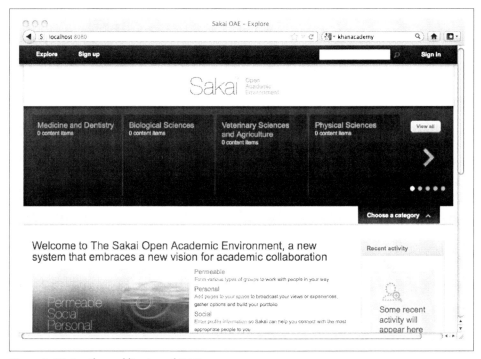

Figure 3-15. Another public view of OAE

The Explore menu on the top left will take you to all publicly available information of a specific type: Content, People, Groups, Courses, and Research Projects. Select People and you'll be taken to search results for all the accounts in the system (see Figure 3-16). There will be two, unless you got all god-like and started creating people like mad. If the accounts have tags or categories associated, these will automatically be suggested as refinements to reduce the list of results.

Figure 3-16. Searching for people shows everyone who has a public profile

Individuals can opt not to be publically listed in the search by changing the Privacy settings of their account. The privacy settings apply to profile information and to lists of content, membership, and contacts. There's no Only me setting for accounts, but visibility can be limited to just Logged in users.

CHAPTER 4

Making the Look and Feel Your Own

The OAE project has been design-led from the outset. Getting the aesthetic right makes the user experience flow more easily. This chapter introduces you to CSS, label display, language localization, modifying the category metadata, and modifying the landing page widget. The technical work is the easy part in many ways. Designing and deciding all the visual and navigational elements of your instance of OAE requires time and expertise. Be sure to bring in a talented designer, and once you do, remember to listen to her.

Configure OAE for CSS, Property, and JavaScript Changes

To make look-and-feel changes, configure the running server to look at the UI code you unzipped in "Building from Source" on page 15. Changes to CSS, labels, and language localizations are all done in the unzipped UI code. When you're happy with your changes, then you can rebundle the system to make the UI permanent.

Ready for some acronyms? Okay. Sakai OAE is built on the Apache Felix implementation of the OSGi framework. It further relies on the Apache Sling OSGi bundles for RESTful implementation of HTTP request handling. To some extent these framework selections derive from an earlier architecture that anticipated full reliance on JSR-170, the Java content repository, to serve all the content needs of Sakai OAE. In pilot deployments, it became apparent that the needs for concurrent reads and writes on a shallow, broad tree structure in Sakai OAE were in contention with how JCR optimized. This brought about the development of the `sparsemapcontent` storage API layer and `solr` indexing to improve performance under heavy load. (See Figure 4-1.)

The view layer is implemented in CSS and JavaScript, with heavy reliance on the jQuery library. Customization handling differs slightly if it's at the CSS and properties layer from if it's at the JavaScript layer.

In order to customize anything, Nakamura needs to know where to look for your customizations. Open a browser to *http://localhost:8080/system/console*. The default username and password are **admin**/**admin**. You are now looking at the dashboard to the guts

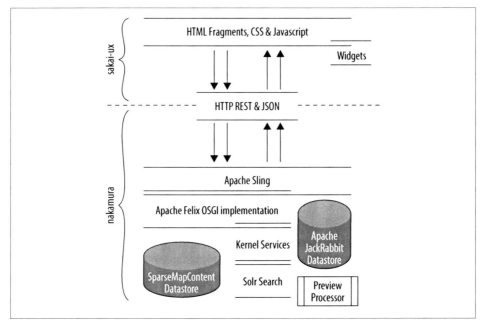

Figure 4-1. Some key OAE technologies in the stack

of the Sakai OAE system. Click the `Configuration` button to get over to the Sling configuration manager. Modules are listed alphabetically. Scroll down until you find the `Apache Sling Filesystem Resource Provider`. Click the plus (+) button to create an entry that overrides the packaged frontend code location.

For `Provider root`, enter:

/dev

For `Filesystem root`, enter:

/Users/*username*/source/sakai-ux/dev

Leave the other values at their defaults and click **Save**. (See Figure 4-2.)When you add a new Resource Provider, the Felix interface doesn't necessarily update immediately to show you the new entry. If you want to confirm that your new entry took, refresh your browser and scroll back down to the `Apache Sling Filesystem Resource Provider`. Under the Filesystem Resource Provider heading you'll see an entry for `org.apache.sling.fsprovider.internal.FsResourceProvider` with a unique suffix string.

Before getting down to real work, do something quick and destructive to show that you have control of the user interface code now.

1. Change to your dev directory:

    cd /Users/*username*/source/sakai-ux/dev

2. Move your *index.html* file to a safe backup copy:

```
mv index.html index.html.bak
```

3. Create a new *index.html* with an unmistakable message:

```
echo I Own the UI > index.html
```

4. Connect to *http://localhost:8080* to see the fruits of your labor (see Figure 4-3).

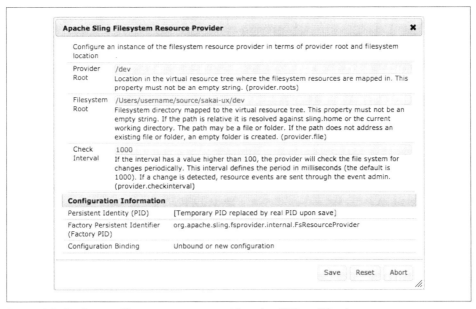

Figure 4-2. Configure a filesystem resource to pick up local UI modifications

Figure 4-3. The user interface is so p0wned

Changes made in HTML files take effect as soon as you connect to OAE.

Now put it all back:

```
mv index.html.bak index.html
```

and reload your browser. Phew. No harm done. If you have done harm, just unzip the frontend code again and rename the directory to match what you put in the Sling console for the Filesystem Resource (e.g., */Users/username/source/sakai-ux*).

When you connect to Sakai OAE now notice that you are the admin user. When you log in as admin to the console, you end up with all possible rights and privileges in the OAE system. To log out, you have to close and restart your browser. Use this knowledge carefully. With great power comes great responsibility.

Close and restart your browser, then create yourself a new user to test with.

Modifying Labels in the User Interface

Most elements displayed in the user interface of Sakai OAE are just labels for variables. Modifying the text displayed is as straightforward as changing the label in the default properties file. The file *default.properties* in *sakai-ux/dev/bundle* contains all the customizable display text in OAE. It's an alphabetically ordered monster of a properties file. For the most part, the variable names match the initial English label values displayed out of the box. As you make changes to *default.properties* keep a copy of the original version around as a reference.

To see it in action, change the heading for *Basic Information* in the user profile section. Login to the web interface at *http://localhost:8080* and expand the My profile section. Notice that the lefthand navigation shows the section heading for the first section as Basic information. Open up the *default.properties* file and modify the display value for PROFILE_BASIC_LABEL. Change:

```
PROFILE_BASIC_LABEL = Basic information
```

to:

```
PROFILE_BASIC_LABEL = Name, email, stuff
```

and save the file. Refresh your browser. The first section under My profile now displays as Name, email, stuff.

Changes you make in *default.properties* are automatically adopted the next time anyone loads a page.

Internationalization and Localization

The display labels in Sakai OAE can not only be customized, they can also be translated and internationalized. Localization property files are stored in *sakai-ux/dev/bundle* alongside the *default.properties* file. Sakai OAE ships with limited translations for Spanish, American and British English, Dutch, Magyar, and Chinese.

A localization file can contain just a subset of labels; it need not exhaustively translate the labels in *default.properties*. As an example, crack open the *en_GB.properties* files in *sakai-ux/dev/bundle*. The only two labels customized out of the box are those containing the word *acknowledgements*. In the States, this word is acceptably spelled *acknowledgments*, whereas in Great Britain only *acknowledgements* is correct.

Start by setting your account language preference to English (United Kingdom).

1. Login at *http://localhost:8080* and select My account from the top-right drop-down list associated with your name.

2. On the Preferences tab, select English (United Kingdom) for Language and click Save changes, as shown in Figure 4-4.

Figure 4-4. My account language settings

The web browser will automatically refresh with the United Kingdom localization. You won't notice many changes. The *Language* listed at the bottom right of your browser screen will update to show you are now set to English (United Kingdom). Modify the properties file to localize a third display label. For our British version of OAE, replace the You menu with the more generic label One. In the file *en_GB.properties* add the line:

YOU = One

and save the file. Order is not meaningful in the properties files, so technically you can place the new label value anywhere. As these grow though, it's good to have the values alphabetized by variable, so drop the new line in at the end of the *en_GB.properties* file.

Refresh your browser and the new menu name *One* displays in place of *You* in the upper-left of the browser screen. (See Figure 4-5.)

Introducing a new localization requires creating a fresh properties file for the region, and also making a modification to add a new option to the My account drop-down list of Languages. The *config.js* file in *sakai-ux/dev/configuration* maintains the Languages drop-down list. This will be your first look at the JavaScript layer of customization in OAE.

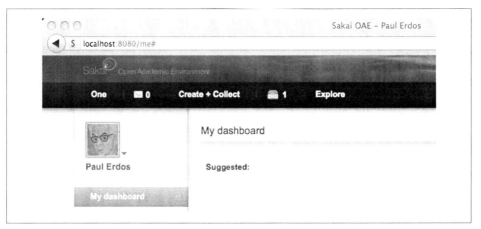

Figure 4-5. UK English menu using the third person plural instead of the second person pronoun

1. Create a new file in *sakai-ux/dev/bundle* with the name *zu_ZA.properties*. *zu-ZA* is the i18n code for the Xhosa language in the South African geographic region.

2. Modify the display label for the *You* menu to the Xhosa word for hello, by adding the following line to your new *zu_ZA.properties* file:

   ```
   YOU = Molo
   ```

3. Change to the *sakai-ux/dev/configuration* directory and take a quick backup of the *config.js* file. It's easy to mess up the JavaScript syntax, and you can accidentally white-bomb your OAE install with a stray semicolon:

   ```
   cp -p config.js config.js.bak
   ```

4. Locate the `Languages` section in the *config.js* file, about line 1511. Add a block for the new localization option:

   ```
   {
   "country": "ZA",
   "language": "zu",
   "displayName": "Xhosa (South Africa)"
   },
   ```

   The Xhosa option will turn up in the position in which you place it relative to the other language options in the menu. Be careful with your brackets and commas as you place it in the list.

5. JavaScript content is eagerly cached in the browser in order to improve the performance of OAE. To see the new localization option, refresh the cache in your browser.

   In Firefox: `Preferences→Advanced→Network`, then in `Cached Web Content` click `Clear Now`. In Safari: `Safari` menu→`Empty Cache→Empty`.

6. Select `My account` from the top-right drop-down list associated with your name, then on the `Preferences` tab, select `Xhosa (South Africa)` for Languages and click `Save changes`. (See Figure 4-6.)

The top-left menu changes from *You* (or *One*) to *Molo*. (See Figure 4-7.)

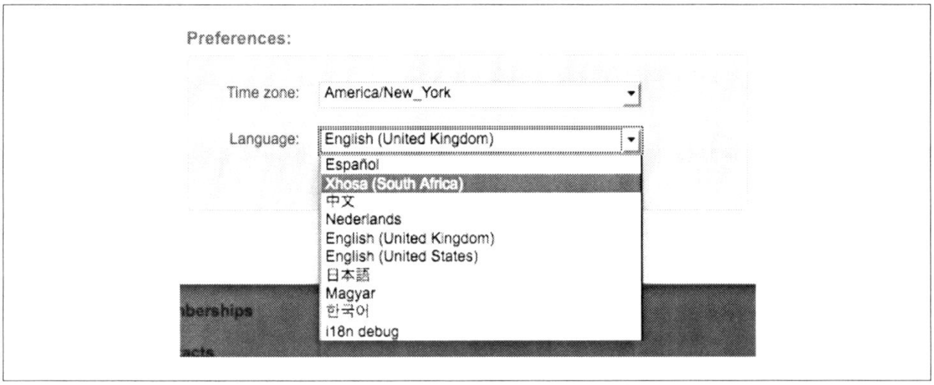

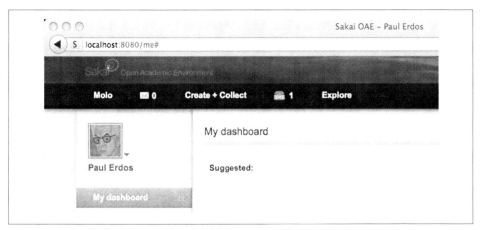

Figure 4-6. *Xhosa Language menu item is added by editing config.js*

If the Xhosa option doesn't turn up, make sure you've saved the *zu_ZA.properties* file and the revised *config.js* file and try refreshing your cache again.

Figure 4-7. *Xhosa South Africa menu using a greeting in lieu of a pronoun*

If you are ever scratching your head for what the underlying label name is for a bit of display text, you can use the special language setting i18n debug to see the labels in place in the UI. In the My account menu, click the Preferences button, then select the last of the language settings, i18n debug. When the window refreshes, all the display text is replaced with the corresponding label names. Before you roll OAE into production, remove the i18n debug option from the Language list. See "Reducing the JavaScript Debug Logging" on page 98 for details on getting production ready.

Changing the CSS: Paint It Pink

Sakai OAE is entirely styled with Cascading Style Sheets. You can customize the look of the system for your local environment by providing your own stylesheets, overriding the selectors with custom properties and values.

The default CSS files for OAE are stored in *sakai-ux/dev/css*. The bulk of the CSS files of interest are in the *sakai* directory under *css*. The two other directories in this location are *FSS* and *lib*. The FSS stylesheets come to OAE from the Fluid project (*http://fluid project.org*), which enables a high level of customization to individuals for accessibility purposes. Inclusion of the Fluid skinning system in Sakai OAE allows people with visual or other impairments to alter the display of OAE, making content accessible to them that might otherwise be unavailable.

In the *lib* directory is a single stylesheet for tweaking the jQuery-based AutoSuggest display.

The styles you'll want to get famliar with are all in *.css* files located in *dev/css/sakai*:

sakai.corev1.css
> The primary stylesheet, providing the main layout for all pages defining columns, content areas, and header areas.

sakai.base.css
> The primary element styling file, all 2,700 lines of it. This is the most important stylesheet in the system. All the *s3d* consolidated styles are defined here. The sections are commented to guide you to what is being styled by the selectors that follow (e.g., global rules, drop-down menus, links, buttons, search boxes). The Mozilla Firebug plug-in (*https://addons.mozilla.org/firefox/addon/firebug/*) is invaluable in picking out the selector names for rules you'd like to change.

main.css
> The aggregating master file. The *main.css* imports the Fluid skinning system base classes, the jQuery AutoSuggest tweak from the local CSS library and a jQuery gritter stylesheet for popping up alert messages. It imports the two key OAE specific stylesheets: *sakai.base.css* and *sakai.components.jq_pager.css*.

sakai.explore.css
> Styles the Search results page, whether reached via the Explore menu or by entering something in the search box. This stylesheet also covers the category and subcategory displays, and the index page (conceptualized as exploring categories from the root). The *sakai.explore.css* file overrides some of the styles defined in *sakai.base.css* and *sakai.corev1.css*.

sakai.create_new_account.css
> Styles the Sign Up page at *http://localhost:8080/register*, overriding the base styles as needed.

sakai.createnew.css

Styles the Create Group, Create Course, and Create Research project pages, over-riding just one base style.

sakai.group.css

Style for group sites, whether a straight up group, a course, or a research project.

sakai.content_profile.css

Styles the content profile pages, overriding the base styles as needed.

sakai.error.css

Styles the 403, 404, and 500 error pages.

The standard for customizing the skin is to add a directory for your own CSS files to the skin directory at *sakai-ux/dev/skins*. You could change the main CSS files, but keeping track across upgrades is really painful. Just start out by doing the right thing right now. You'll thank yourself later.

For the directory name, pick a convenient shorthand to represent your institution. Three to five characters is a good rule of thumb. These examples use the shorthand *myedu*, which should be replaced. Under *sakai-ux/dev/skins/myedu* create a new *.css* file with the name *myedu.skin.css* and an *images* directory .

The reason you can pull this off is that CSS uses a single namespace. The upside is that if you use the right name for a CSS style, you override the default style without any additional effort. The downside is that it's one namespace and it's not totally docu-mented. The safest thing to do (and the standard practice in the OAE community) is to prefix any new style name with your institution's shorthand name. A new link type styling for your institution would be named `myedu.newlink` rather than simply `new link`. Even if `newlink` doesn't exist as a global style today it might be added in the future, introducing strange and undocumented pain later on:

```
sakai-ux/dev
  /css
     /FSS
     /lib
     /sakai
  /skins
     /default
         skin.css
     /myedu
         myedu.skin.css
         /images
```

In your new *myedu.skin.css* file add the contents:

```
/* Pink Links */
a {
        color: #E00333;
}
.s3d-add_another_location {
        color: #E0039C;
}
```

```
.s3d-regular-links, span.s3d-regular-links, .s3d-regular-links a,
button.s3d-regular-links, .s3d-regular-links button,
.contentauthoring_cell_element a {
        color: #E683bc;
}
.s3d-widget-links, span.s3d-widget-links, .s3d-widget-links a,
button.s3d-widget-links, .s3d-widget-links button {
        color: #E683bc;
}
.s3d-regular-light-links, .s3d-regular-light-links a,
.s3d-regular-light-links button {
        color: #E58EC4 !important;
}
.s3d-content-type-link a {
        color: #EFB3D2;
}
.s3d-tab-active a {
        background-color: #E00FFF !important;
        color: #000 !important;
        border-color: #E00DDD #E00DDD #E00EEE;
}
/* new path used when creating pages */
.content_container .new_page_path {
        color: #E00999;
}
/* Vicious Selector Ordering */
a.s3d-regular-links,
.s3d-regular-links a,
button.s3d-regular-links,
.s3d-regular-links button,
button.s3d-link-button,
.s3d-button.s3d-overlay-button,
.addarea_contents_list_item,
#selecttemplate_container h2,
#selecttemplate_preview_dialog_container h2 {
    color:#E7068c !important;
}
```

This CSS takes each of the link assocated selectors in *sakai.base.css* and shifts them from the blue range to the much more attractive pink and magenta range. The new colors won't take effect though until you direct OAE to the custom CSS file instead of the default one.

This brings us to the *config_custom.js* file for the first time. The *config_custom.js* is stored in the same location as *config.js*, but is a much smaller file, specifically intended for taking local configuration information. (It was a bit of hacking around to add a language set to *config.js* in the localization section at "Internationalization and Localization" on page 44.)

Head over to *sakai-ux/dev/configuration* and take a look at the contents of config_cus tom.js. It has a grand total of 34 lines, none of which are active out-of-the-box. Uncomment the config.skinCSS setting and edit the path to point to your new skin:

```
config.skinCSS = ["/dev/skins/myedu/myedu.skin.css"];
```

Save the *config_custom.js* file, then empty your browser cache and reload the page (see Figure 4-8). Because this change is to a JavaScript file, it's necessary to flush the browser cache and reload. If you want to make subsequent changes to your CSS, you can just reload the page from here on in because CSS files are not cached.

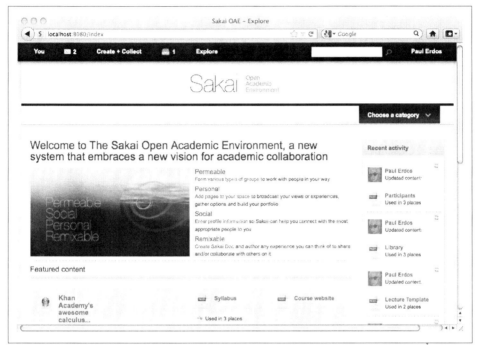

Figure 4-8. If your paper were a full-color display these links would look like flamingos

To see that in action, paint the links black now. Replace the contents of your *myedu.skin.css* with the below:

```
/* Black & Grey Links */
a {
        color: #000000;
}
.s3d-add_another_location {
        color: #696969;
}
.s3d-regular-links, span.s3d-regular-links, .s3d-regular-links a,
button.s3d-regular-links, .s3d-regular-links button,
.contentauthoring_cell_element a {
        color: #D3D3D3;
}
.s3d-widget-links, span.s3d-widget-links, .s3d-widget-links a,
button.s3d-widget-links, .s3d-widget-links button {
        color: #D3D3D3;
}
.s3d-regular-light-links, .s3d-regular-light-links a,
```

```
.s3d-regular-light-links button {
        color: #COCOCO !important;
}
.s3d-content-type-link a {
        color: #DCDCDC;
}
.s3d-tab-active a {
        background-color: #2F4F4F !important;
        color: #000 !important;
        border-color: #778899 #778899 #708090;
}
/* new path used when creating pages */
.content_container .new_page_path {
        color: #696969;
}
/* Vicious Selector Ordering */
a.s3d-regular-links,
.s3d-regular-links a,
button.s3d-regular-links,
.s3d-regular-links button,
button.s3d-link-button,
.s3d-button.s3d-overlay-button,
.addarea_contents_list_item,
#selecttemplate_container h2,
#selecttemplate_preview_dialog_container h2 {
    color:#696969 !important;
}
```

Once you save the *myedu.skin.css* file, do a simple refresh in your browser to see the changes take effect.

You'll notice that in both set ups, there is some fairly vicious selector override material at the end of the file. Because order matters in CSS, sometimes the color you expect won't load because a subsequently defined style is being applied (thus the *cascading* in CSS). The selector ordering override is less than ideal, but it gets the job done.

The other less than ideal item to call out here is the heavy use of the rule `!important` . The OAE developers' guidelines states fairly clearly that "!important should be avoided where possible." In practice, it's the big hammer everyone pulls out when a style just won't override. Try to avoid it, and if you can't avoid it, concede and hit the stylesheet with `!important`.

The OAE Widget SDK has some good CSS guides and guidelines in development on the Sakai Project website at *http://oae-widgets.sakaiproject.org/sdk/codestyleguide/css*. That's a good starting point. If you get stumped, the community is always open to questions in IRC and on its mailing lists. Check http://oae-widgets.sakaiproject.org/sdk/contact (*oae-widgets.sakaiproject.org/sdk/contact*) for pointers on where to find live human beings who might be able to help.

Flip the look and feel back to the default by recommenting the `config.skinCSS` line in your *config_custom.js* file. Refresh your browser cache and everything will go back to an aesthetically pleasing state.

Changing Drop-Down Menus

In some places, it may not be sufficient to change the display labels or the color scheme. You might need to change the number of options presented in a drop-down list, or even change the variable name used in the *default.properties* and localized *.properties* files. In the current version of OAE, you can reduce the number of options presented in a drop-down list, but not expand it.

The `Role/position` listing is a good example, as this is a list often requiring modification to match local vocabulary. Login and navigate to your account's `My profile Name, email, stuff` section (this will still be the `Basic information` section if you didn't change it in section "Modifying Labels in the User Interface" on page 44). The `Role/position` drop-down list provides nine options by default: Academic related staff, Academic staff, Assistant staff, Graduate student, Undergraduate student, Non-academic staff, Postgraduate student, Research staff, and Other. Each of these has a corresponding variable name and value defined in the *default.properties* file in *sakai-ux/dev/bundle*. Just as with changing the `Basic information` display label to `Name, email, stuff`, you can change any of the display values in the drop-down list by just modifying the value associated with a variable name:

```
PROFILE_BASIC_ROLE_ACADEMIC_RELATED_STAFF_LABEL = Academic related staff
PROFILE_BASIC_ROLE_ACADEMIC_STAFF_LABEL = Academic staff
PROFILE_BASIC_ROLE_ASSISTENT_STAFF_LABEL = Assistant staff
PROFILE_BASIC_ROLE_GRADUATE_STUDENT_LABEL = Graduate student
PROFILE_BASIC_ROLE_LABEL = Role/position
PROFILE_BASIC_ROLE_NON_ACADEMIC_STAFF_LABEL = Non-academic staff
PROFILE_BASIC_ROLE_OTHER_LABEL = Other
PROFILE_BASIC_ROLE_POSTGRADUATE_STUDENT_LABEL = Postgraduate student
PROFILE_BASIC_ROLE_RESEARCH_STAFF_LABEL = Research staff
PROFILE_BASIC_ROLE_UNDERGRADUATE_STUDENT_LABEL = Undergraduate student
```

However, it may be that these roles just don't make any sense in your environment. If remapping the provided labels isn't sufficient for you, then it's time to dig a little deeper into customization. Change over to the *sakai-ux/dev/configuration* directory, and take another look at the *config.js* file. This is the same file where you added a language choice to the localization menu in section "Internationalization and Localization" on page 44 This time we're going to keyhole in on the Roles dropdown list. About line 309 is the entry for the Role/position section of the Profile:

```
"role": {
  "label": "__MSG__PROFILE_BASIC_ROLE_LABEL__",
  "required": false,
  "display": true,
  "type": "select",
  "select_elements": {
    "academic_related_staff":
        "__MSG__PROFILE_BASIC_ROLE_ACADEMIC_RELATED_STAFF_LABEL__",
    "academic_staff":
        "__MSG__PROFILE_BASIC_ROLE_ACADEMIC_STAFF_LABEL__",
    "assistent_staff":
```

```
            "__MSG__PROFILE_BASIC_ROLE_ASSISTENT_STAFF_LABEL__",
        "graduate_student":
            "__MSG__PROFILE_BASIC_ROLE_GRADUATE_STUDENT_LABEL__",
        "undergraduate_student":
            "__MSG__PROFILE_BASIC_ROLE_UNDERGRADUATE_STUDENT_LABEL__",
        "non_academic_staff":
            "__MSG__PROFILE_BASIC_ROLE_NON_ACADEMIC_STAFF_LABEL__",
        "postgraduate_student":
            "__MSG__PROFILE_BASIC_ROLE_POSTGRADUATE_STUDENT_LABEL__",
        "research_staff":
            "__MSG__PROFILE_BASIC_ROLE_RESEARCH_STAFF_LABEL__",
        "other":
            "__MSG__PROFILE_BASIC_ROLE_OTHER_LABEL__"
    }
},
```

The label name from *default.properties* appears in *config.js* prefixed with a double underscore, the flag MSG and another double underscore, then suffixed with a final double underscore. This is the convention Sakai OAE uses for identifying display values which should be localized. Any string bracketed by __MSG__ and __ gets checked against the active account's language setting. If the variable has a corresponding entry in the language specific *.properties* file then that value is displayed, otherwise the entry from *default.properties* is taken.

In *config.js* you can change the label names and you can reduce the size of the display list. What you can't do, without going a lot deeper into the system, is change the internal names of the options (e.g., 'academic_related_staff,' 'academic_staff').

We'll do both as examples, correcting that confounded spelling error in the label name for PROFILE_BASIC_ROLE_ASSISTENT_STAFF_LABEL and dropping the Other option from the overall list. Again, take a back up of the *config.js* file before you start work. You can always unpack another clean copy from the ZIP file you downloaded, but having one handy makes it easy to check your work and revert if something goes wildly off kilter. Part of being a good technologist is managing your own distress when you mess a system up.

Modify the assistant staff line to correct the spelling error in just the parameter key:

```
    "assistent_staff": "__MSG__PROFILE_BASIC_ROLE_ASSISTANT_STAFF_LABEL__",
```

Sadly, we can't also correct the internal value from assistent_staff to assistant_staff. Something deeper in the system is expecting *assistent* to be consistently misspelled.

Remove the line for the "other" entry and the preceding comma, so that "research_staff" is the last item in the list. Save the *config.js* file.

Before you finish the *assistent* spelling correction pop back over to your web browser, clear your cache and refresh the My profile screen (see Figure 4-9). There are two things to notice: first, the Other option is now gone from the Role/position drop-down list. Anyone who had selected *Other* as their role will continue to have that role associated with their profile, but no one will be able to select it afresh. The value persists on the backend, even though you've removed it from the list of options on the display end.

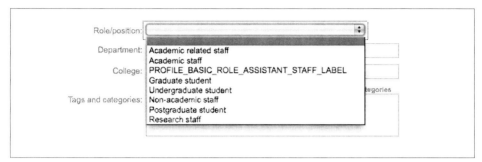

Figure 4-9. Distinctly half-finished modification to the Roles drop-down

The other thing to note is that the drop-down list now displays the raw label string `PROFILE_BASIC_ROLE_ASSISTENT_STAFF_LABEL` where the more pleasant `Assistant staff` should display. If the JavaScript provides a variable name for which there is no entry in an appropriate *.properties* file, OAE just delivers the unmatched label to the user interface.

Open up the *default.properties* file in *sakai-ux/dev/bundle* and change it to the following:

```
PROFILE_BASIC_ROLE_ASSISTANT_STAFF_LABEL = Assistant staff
```

Save this file and refresh the `My profile` view in your browser. This time the change will take without requiring that you refresh the browser cache. Cache refreshes are needed only when you modify a JavaScript file.

Refreshing Cache

Many of the OAE frontend developers keep caching turned off in their browsers while they work on the frontend in order to reduce the annoyance of hunting a bug that is just in an inconsistent cache state. Keep in mind that your users won't be configured to always reconsult the server for fresh code (indeed you wouldn't want them to; it would needlessly load up your server). When troubleshooting a real person's problems, always make emptying the browser cache the first step in diagnosis.

Why would you want to change a label name if you can't modify the internal reference? Changing the label names can reduce confusion if you want the display values to be maintained by non-technical or minimally technical members of staff. The OAE development team thought the parameter names were a good idea when they got started on the profile functions, but that doesn't mean they're intuitive in your environment. By making the key names closer to your organization's internal vocabulary you can move the decision making out to the people who are responsible for those decisions, rather than gating everything on someone with appropriate operating system privileges. Those privileges are for solving technical problems, not for creating bottlenecks. Of course, if you're a power hungry system admin feel free to keep this material obscured from the prying eyes of mere mortals.

There is an equally compelling argument in favor of keeping a gatekeeper in the middle who controls the *.properties* files: every change you make to the JavaScript files today will have to be maintained by the technical staff across upgrades of the code. If you have a solid code control, build management, and QA process in your IT department, then it can make sense to customize the parameter names. If you are likely to have to recode these JavaScript message strings by hand each time you upgrade, it's probably better to leave the JavaScript as close to the out-of-the-box version as possible.

Categories

The public browsing views of Sakai OAE provide visitors with a view into the people, research, and groups at your institution. Any element of OAE that's been marked public and had a category assigned will turn up here (*http://localhost:8080/categories*), ordered according to the categories tree. Like the values for the `Role/position` drop-down list, two levels of customization can be done here. In the *default.properties* file, the display values can be modified. In the *config.js* file, options can be removed and parameter key names can be changed. Unlike other parameters that are more tightly bound to the backend, display categories and subcategories can also be added as well as removed. The categories are one of the highest stakes configurations you'll make to the Sakai OAE system, as this is fundamentally an identity activity for your institution. When visitors land at your OAE instance how do you want to guide them through the publicly available materials? When students decide to make their essays public, how do you want them to characterize their work?

In order to see the effects of category changes, whip up the *Partial Derivative for Dreamers* course, just as you did in Chapter 2 and assign it the category `Medicine & Dentistry >> Pre-clinical Medicine`. Make sure to set the course to be discoverable by the public, so it turns up in the public *Explore* space.

Start with one quick improvement to the defaults provided when you install OAE: removing excess verbiage in the *Other* listings. The hierarchy is built into the label keys; it need not be displayed to people as if they, too, were computers.

In the directory *sakai-ux/dev/bundle*, edit *default.properties*. Update a couple of the *other* category display values to simply say `Other`. For example change `Others in Medicine and Dentistry` and `Others in Biological Sciences` to just `Other`.

From:

```
MEDICINE_AND_DENTISTRY_OTHERS = Others in Medicine and Dentistry
...
BIOLOGICAL_SCIENCES_OTHERS = Others in Biological Sciences
```

to:

```
MEDICINE_AND_DENTISTRY_OTHERS = Other
...
BIOLOGICAL_SCIENCES_OTHERS = Other
```

Save the file and direct your browser to the public browsing page at *http://localhost:8080/categories*. Clicking through on the `Medicine and Dentistry` or `Biological Scien ces` categories will now show the last subcategory listed as simply `Other`. Click on the `Other` section in `Biological Sciences` and the URL shows that you're still in the *Biological Sciences* category area, as does the lefthand navigation. As subcategories are consistently displayed in the context of their parent, you can safely shorten the display names to take advantage of that context.

In the current version of OAE, the category infrastructure is pretty resilient, it just hasn't had a pretty configuration interface written yet. You can remove categories and subcategories, change internal names as well as display names and the system automatically detects your new scheme. Removing a category wholesale, and introducing a new one, doesn't present a significant challenge.

To remove a category, open up our old friend, the *config.js* file in *sakai-ux/dev/configuration*. All the display JavaScript for the categories is in the `Directory:` section, starting about line 1009. To remove the entire "Medicine and Dentistry" category, delete all the lines from `medicineanddentistry` down to but not including the next category header, `biologicalsciences`. To remove the single `botany` subcategory from the *Biological Sciences* section, delete the three lines for that subcategory:

```
botany: {
    title: "__MSG__BOTANY__"
},
```

You want to end up with a Directory section with the first 10 lines:

```
Directory: {
    biologicalsciences: {
        title: "__MSG__BIOLOGICAL_SCIENCES__",
            children: {
                biology: {
                    title: "__MSG__BIOLOGY__"
                },
                zoology: {
                    title: "__MSG__ZOOLOGY__"
                },
```

Before adding anything new in, test this out. Save the *config.js* file, empty your browser cache and reload the browsing page at *http://localhost:8080/categories*. The `Medicine` and `Dentistry` section is now gone. Clicking in to the `Biological Sciences` section shows that the `Botany` subcategory is gone as well.

If you search for a course tagged with one of the categories we've removed you'll find that it now displays with the confusing tag: `false >> false`. Select `Courses` from the `Explore` menu and you'll see the *Partial Derivatives for Dreamers* course with this false tag value. Click on the tag and the URL will show an attempt to search with the original category values, but the system will deliver a 404 error. As mentioned the category subsystem is resilient, but it's not exactly robust. When you first deploy Sakai OAE it's best to start with a small selection of categories and subcategories, then expand, rather than starting broad and having to sort out how to manage category removals after they've been used.

Adding a category requires entries is both *config.js* and *default.properties* files. When you create a new category, prefix the internal name and the label key with the short term for your institution. This will prevent potential name clashes down the line. Like CSS style names, all label keys exist in a single namespace. If a future version of OAE introduces a parameter key you're already using it will be a pain to make the name localization at that time. Do the right thing now. Your future self will thank you.

Let's say your university has introduced a new Nanotechnology department. The first step is to add it to the `Directory` section in *config.js*. The categories display in the same order they are listed in JavaScript. The provost wants to feature the nanotechnology category, so add it directly after `Directory` and before the `biologicalsciences` entry. The first 14 lines of your new Directory section should look like this:

```
Directory: {
    myedunanotech: {
        title: "__MSG__MYEDU_NANOTECH__",
            children: {
                myedunanotechbio: {
                    title: "__MSG__MYEDU_NANOTECH_BIO__"
                },
                myedunanotechsynth: {
                    title: "__MSG__MYEDU_NANOTECH_SYNTH__"
                }
            }
    },
    biologicalsciences: {
        title: "__MSG__BIOLOGICAL_SCIENCES__",
```

Now, enter the corresponding parameter keys and values to your `default.properties` file on */source/sakai-ux/dev/bundles*. The parameter key is the `title` value stripped of the leading `__MSG__` and the trailing `__`. Add the following lines to your *default.properties*:

```
MYEDU_NANOTECH = Nanotechnology
MYEDU_NANOTECH_BIO = Nanobiotechnology
MYEDU_NANOTECH_SYNTH = Synthetic Nanotechnology
```

Save the *config.js* and *default.properties* files, empty your browser's cache and reload the Categories page (see Figure 4-10). The Nanotechnology category is now the first box on the All categories page.

Figure 4-10. Brand spanking new department of Nanotechnology

Troubleshooting

Modifying the *config.js* file in general, and the directory section in particular, is a bit of tricky business. Here are a couple of troubleshooting tips:

Nothing changes
Always remember to empty your browser cache. Sakai OAE caches eagerly in order to improve performance. Make sure the language setting in your Sakai OAE account matches the *.properties* file you're working with on disk. Set your account to a language with minimal or no localization in its corresponding *.properties* file in order to make sure you're picking up the display values from *default.properties*.

An all-cap string appears in the web browser
Double check the correspondence between the title value in your *config.js* file and the parameter key in your *default.properties* file. Transposed letters are particularly hard to see when you're in all caps in a fixed font. Trying doing a strict copy and paste from one file to the other, remembering to strip out the prefixing `__MSG__` and trailing `__` from the *config.js* title before adding it to *default.properties*. Next, double check the format of the title value in *config.js*. If there are single underscores where there should be double underscores OAE will display the parameter without substituting the display value.

A weird mix of a display value and an all capital string appears in the web browser
You may have double underscores in the title value where you meant to have single underscores. Sakai OAE parses the key parameter as whatever is sandwiched between the prefix `__MSG__` and the next following double underscore, then just coughs up everything that comes after it.

A display value shows in the web browser, but it's not the one you expect
> Double check that you haven't accidentally reused a parameter key already in use. For example, if your library studies school has a subcategory key of `COLLECTIONS` it will clash with the OAE key for localizing the name of the *Collections* functionally. The standard practice is to prefix your institution's label keys with a short form of the institution name in order to reduce namespace collisions (e.g. `MYEDU_COLLEC TIONS` instead of `COLLECTIONS`).

Everything's gone white (the tragic white-bomb)
> If nothing will load in the browser, not even an error page, then you've got a syntax error in your *config.js* file. Restore a clean back up of the *config.js* file and start over. It's probably a stray comma or a missing bracket. This is one of the challenges of working directly in the JavaScript. Future versions of OAE will have a configuration tool to simplify the category management process. In the meantime, tread carefully and test like crazy before you touch your production system.

Change the Landing Page

When people first visit Sakai OAE, the landing page introduces some key themes about OAE. The area that displays the Permeable/Social/Personal/Remixable image is actually a *widget*, a small block of customized code that runs inside the Sakai OAE environment. In order to start customizing a widget, OAE needs to know where to find the revised widget. Just like the CSS and JavaScript file location indication done in section "Configure OAE for CSS, Property, and JavaScript Changes" on page 41, the widget location is indicated with a new Filesystem Resource Provider.

Open your browser to *http://localhost:8080/system/console* and login again with the default username and password **admin**/**admin**. Click the `Configuration` button to get over to the Sling configuration manager. Click the plus (+) button next to `Apache Sling Filesystem Resource Provider` to create an entry overriding the devwidget location.

For `Provider root`, enter: **/devwidgets**

For `Filesystem root`, enter: **/Users/*username*/source/sakai-ux/devwidgets**

Leave the other values at their defaults and click `Save`. Refresh your browser and scroll back down to the `Apache Sling Filesystem Resource Provider`. Under the Filesystem Resource Provider heading there are now two entries for `org.apache.sling.fspro vider.internal.FsResourceProvider` with unique sufffix strings: one for your local *dev* location and now another for your local *devwidgets* location.

The welcome screen widget is located in *sakai-ux/devwidgets/welcome*.

In the *welcome.html* file, substitute a new image for the landing page:

```
<img src="/devwidgets/welcome/images/sakai_default.png" alt="__MSG__KEYWORDS__">
```

change to:

```
<img src="http://farm8.staticflickr.com/7013/6620145495_c5208b58de_n_d.jpg"
alt="__MSG__KEYWORDS__">
```

In the *default.properties* file, provide some new keywords for the alternate text for screen readers:

```
KEYWORDS = Sakai: Permeable, Social, Personal, Remixable
```

change to:

```
KEYWORDS = St. Paul's doorway image courtesy of Ian Dolphin, used under the Creative
Commons Attribution, Noncommercial, No Derivative works license.
```

Also change the first set of display text and link:

```
WELCOME_ITEM1_TITLE = Permeable
WELCOME_ITEM1_LINK = /create#l=group
WELCOME_ITEM1_LINK_TEXT = Form various types of groups
WELCOME_ITEM1_OTHER_TEXT = to work with people in your way
```

change to:

```
WELCOME_ITEM1_TITLE = Open
WELCOME_ITEM1_LINK = /categories
WELCOME_ITEM1_LINK_TEXT = Explore
WELCOME_ITEM1_OTHER_TEXT = all the public work at our institution
```

Fnally, make a quick and dirty change to make this first link active for anyone who visits OAE, not just to people who are currently logged in. In *welcome.html*, modify the two *if* statements associated with the first welcome link to always be true by changing {if !anon} to {if true}.

This section of code will now look like the following:

```
<h2>__MSG__WELCOME_ITEM1_TITLE__</h2>
{if true}
    {if '__MSG__WELCOME_ITEM1_LINK__'.substr(0,1) === '#'}
        <button class="s3d-link-button"
                data-trigger="${'__MSG__WELCOME_ITEM1_LINK__'.substr(1)}">
    {else}
        <a class="s3d-regular-links" href="__MSG__WELCOME_ITEM1_LINK__">
    {/if}
{else}
    <span class="s3d-regular-links">
{/if}
__MSG__WELCOME_ITEM1_LINK_TEXT__
{if true}
    {if '__MSG__WELCOME_ITEM1_LINK__'.substr(0,1) === '#'}
        </button>
    {else}
        </a>
    {/if}
{else}
    </span>
```

```
{/if}
<span> __MSG__WELCOME_ITEM1_OTHER_TEXT__</span>
```

Sign out of OAE (if you're signed in) and refresh the landing page at *http://localhost: 8080*. (See Figure 4-11.)

Figure 4-11. The revised landing page widget, with a lovely shot of a doorway in Hull, England

Changing the Sign Up and Error pages

The Sign Up page and the various error pages can be modified using the approaches from this chapter (see Table 4-1). To modify or localize the display labels, modify your account language to i18n debug and access the corresponding URL. The all-cap labels that render in i18n debug mode can have their corresponding display values changed in *default.properties* for the general case, and in the language specific *.properties* file in the localized cases. Styles can be overriden with local CSS styles per section "Configure OAE for CSS, Property, and JavaScript Changes" on page 41, and if necessary, the whole HTML page can be customized. If you do reach into the HTML, be sure to have a code control process in place so subsequent upgrades of the OAE software don't overwrite your hard work.

Table 4-1. Customization Reference for Sign Up and Error Files

Page	URL	HTML	CSS
Sign Up	http://localhost:8080/register	sakai-ux/dev/create_new_account.html	sakai-ux/dev/css/sakai/sakai.create_new_account.css
Access forbidden	http://localhost:8080/dev/403.html	sakai-ux/dev/403.html	sakai-ux/dev/css/sakai/sakai.error.css
Page not found	http://localhost:8080/dev/404.html	sakai-ux/dev/404.html	sakai-ux/dev/css/sakai/sakai.error.css
Internal Server Error	http://localhost:8080/dev/500.html	sakai-ux/dev/500.html	sakai-ux/dev/css/sakai/sakai.error.css

One thing that can't be changed is the recaptcha inclusion in the Sign Up page. While it can be removed as such from the HTML page associated with registration, the user creation kernel services expect a captcha, and won't create a user account without one. (See Figure 4-12 for the error message.)

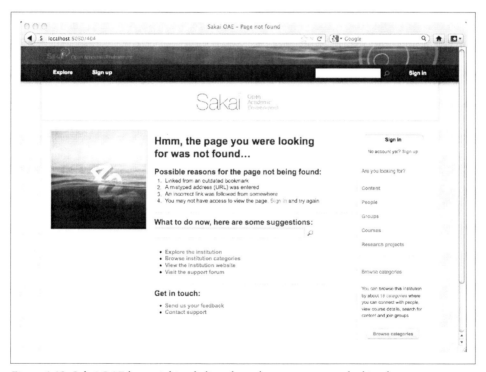

Figure 4-12. Sakai OAE has a sinking feeling about that page you were looking for

Rebundle OAE

When you're ready to commit to your interface changes, rebundle the OAE code into a single deployable jar:

1. Shut down any running instance of OAE.

2. Change into your frontend code directory and rebuild the code to use your customized files:

   ```
   cd source/sakai-ux
   mvn clean install
   ```

   This will take about a minute to complete, and produces a new *.jar* file in your local Maven repository corresponding to the UX.

3. Change into your backend code directory and rebundle the full system. The bundle parameter directs maven to wrap up the jars insteading of rebuilding them all:

   ```
   cd source/nakamura
   mvn -Pbundle clean install
   ```

   This rebundling will take about five minutes. When it completes, you'll have a new nakamura *.jar* file in your *nakamura/app/target* directory. Calling the *tools/ run_production.sh* script on *nix or *tools\run_debug.bat* on Windows will pull up this new jar with the customizations built in to it.

To sanity check your rebuilt OAE in development and confirm that it properly includes the intended customizations, just copy it to a new directory on your development machine and fire it up, being mindful to shut down any other instance of OAE first.

In development, use the `File System Resource` settings to direct the OAE instance at your local dev and devwidgets directories. In stage, test against a freshly deployed *.jar*, with the dev and devwidget materials built in, then deploy that wholly contained jar out to production.

CHAPTER 5

LDAP Integration

Sakai OAE is effective on its own, but it also functions as one element in a campus technology ecosystem. The first step in integrating OAE with other services on campus is setting it up for your school's authentication and authorization environment. Authentication and authorization integration bring OAE into the university fold. Though OAE provides an authentication subsystem, one of your first goals should be to hook accounts up with central services. This is less exciting from the OAE alone perspective. It gets very exciting when you hook up an OAE widget to another university system. Like magic both systems share a list of users, because they're both looking to the same authoritative university source.

This chapter takes you through the process of integrating OAE to a very small, very local open source LDAP installation. This toy integration will give you a handle on how account and authentication management works in the OAE context. Once you've mastered this, you can negotiate meaningfully with your LDAP administrator on how best to roll university authentication into OAE.

While single sign on systems are not directly addressed in this chapter, several have been written, including a CAS integration at University of California, Berkeley, and an OpenSSO integration at New York University. The principles of authentication integration are similar. Working through the LDAP integration can provide a launching pad for other authentication work.

These examples target Linux and other *nix environments. The specifics will differ slightly on Windows.

Set Up a Mini LDAP Instance

In order to be able to watch all layers of your LDAP integration, it's useful to install your own LDAP instance. By no means should you use the instructions in this chapter to configure a production LDAP. Though the open source software used here is production-worthy, this book can't cover the important security and privacy implications of deploying university-wide LDAP.

OpenDJ

OpenDJ is an open source LDAP directory service, including a high performance, highly available, secure directory server with built-in multi-master data replication. It is pretty easy to install and configure. A key factor in choosing it for these examples, OpenDJ runs on any platform that supports Java 6.

You can find more information about the OpenDJ project at *http://opendj.forgerock .org/*.

1. From *http://www.forgerock.org/opendj.html* download the ZIP file for OpenDJ 2.4.5 and unzip the file.
2. For Unix and Linux use the *setup* script.

   For Windows, *setup.bat* script.

   On Mac, double-click on the `QuickSetup.app` application.
3. Select `Install New Server Instance`.
4. Install to the location */Users/username* in a directory called *OpenDJ*

   With hostname `localhost.local`

   LDAP listener port `1389`

   Administrator Connector Port `4444`

   For LDAP Secure Access select `disabled`

   Root User DN `cn=Directory Manager`

   Password set to `password`
5. Select `This will be a stand alone server`.
6. Directory Base DN `dc=example,dc=com`

   For Directory Data, select `Only Create Base Entry (dc=example, dc=com)`.
7. For both the Server Runtime Settings and the Import Runtime Settings, leave them set to `Use Default`.
8. Leave `Start Server when Configuration has Completed` checked and click Finish to install and set the intitial directory tree.

These settings are the equivalent of the command line:

```
/Users/username/OpenDJ/setup \
        --cli \
        --baseDN dc=example,dc=com \
        --addBaseEntry \
        --ldapPort 1389 \
        --adminConnectorPort 4444 \
        --rootUserDN cn=Directory\ Manager \
        --rootUserPassword password \
        --no-prompt \
        --noPropertiesFile
```

Once it completes installing, hit the command line to poke it and make sure it's alive:

OpenDJ-2.4.5/bin/status

For `Administrator user bind DN`, accept the default of `cn=Directory Manager`. For `password`, enter the string `password`, as set during installation.

The response should look like:

```
            --- Server Status ---
Server Run Status:      Started
Open Connections:       1

            --- Server Details ---
Host Name:              localhost.local
Administrative Users:   cn=Directory Manager
Installation Path:      /Users/username/OpenDJ-2.4.5
Version:                OpenDJ 2.4.5
Java Version:           1.6.0_29
Administration Connector: Port 4444 (LDAPS)

            --- Connection Handlers ---
Address:Port : Protocol : State
-------------:----------:---------
--           : LDIF     : Disabled
0.0.0.0:161  : SNMP     : Disabled
0.0.0.0:636  : LDAPS    : Disabled
0.0.0.0:1389 : LDAP     : Enabled
0.0.0.0:1689 : JMX      : Disabled

            --- Data Sources ---
Base DN:    dc=example,dc=com
Backend ID: userRoot
Entries:    1
Replication: Disabled
```

Create some users. Put the following contents in a file named *importTestUsers.ldif*. This ldif file can be downloaded from the O'Reilly website for this book at http://shop.oreilly.com/product/0636920023241.do. (*http://shop.oreilly.com/product/0636920023241.do*)

```
dn: dc=example,dc=com
objectClass: domain
objectClass: top
dc: example

dn: ou=People,dc=example,dc=com
objectClass: organizationalunit
objectClass: top
ou: People

dn: uid=testy,ou=People,dc=example,dc=com
objectClass: person
objectClass: inetorgperson
objectClass: organizationalperson
```

```
objectClass: top
description: This is a terrible test account to be timely terminated.
uid: testy
userPassword: ldap_password
initials: TT
givenName: Testy
cn: Testy McTesterson
sn: McTesterson
mail: testymctesterson@example.edu

dn: uid=paul,ou=People,dc=example,dc=com
objectClass: person
objectClass: inetorgperson
objectClass: organizationalperson
objectClass: top
description: This is the description for Paul Erdos.
uid: paul
userPassword: ldap_password
initials: PE
givenName: Paul
cn: Paul Erdos
sn: Erdos
mail: paulerdos@example.edu

dn: uid=stefan,ou=People,dc=example,dc=com
objectClass: person
objectClass: inetorgperson
objectClass: organizationalperson
objectClass: top
description: This is the description for Stefan Burr.
uid: stefan
userPassword: ldap_password
initials: SB
givenName: Stefan
cn: Stefan Burr
sn: Burr
mail: stefanburr@example.edu

dn: uid=phyllis,ou=People,dc=example,dc=com
objectClass: person
objectClass: inetorgperson
objectClass: organizationalperson
objectClass: top
description: This is the description for Phyllis Chinn.
uid: phyllis
userPassword: ldap_password
initials: PC
givenName: Phyllis
cn: Phyllis Chinn
sn: Chinn
mail: phyllischinn@example.edu
```

Load these users up with the command-line importer, from the directory */Users/user name/OpenDJ/OpenDJ-2.4.5/bin/*:

```
./import-ldif
 --port 4444
 --hostname localhost
 --bindDN "cn=Directory Manager"
 --bindPassword password
 --includeBranch dc=example,dc=com
 --backendID userRoot
 --ldifFile /absolute/path/to/importTestUsers.ldif
```

You're looking for a message like the following, to know that the ldif file import suc-cesfully imported the four user directory entries in the *importTestUsers.ldif* file:

```
severity="NOTICE" msgCount=16 msgID=8847454 message="Processed 4 entries, imported 4,
skipped 0, rejected 0 and migrated 0 in 0 seconds (average rate 9.6/sec)"
```

Check your LDAP directory server and the accuracy of the import by running a search at the command line. The ldapsearch utility is in the directory */Users/username/OpenDJ/ OpenDJ-2.4.5/bin/*:

```
./ldapsearch --hostname localhost --port 1389 --basedn "dc=example,dc=com" \
--binddn "uid=testy,ou=People,dc=example,dc=com" \
--bindPassword ldap_password "uid=testy"
```

If everything has worked correctly, you'll see the LDAP entry for the user Testy McTes-terson. We're going to do bad things to Testy, that's why he's testy. Notice that the password used in this search command is the `ldap_password` as set for the account in the import file, and it differs from the Directory Manager password created when the directory was installed:

```
dn: uid=testy,ou=People,dc=example,dc=com
initials: TT
objectClass: person
objectClass: inetorgperson
objectClass: organizationalperson
objectClass: top
givenName: Testy
uid: testy
description: This is a terrible test account to be timely terminated.
cn: Testy McTesterson
sn: McTesterson
userPassword: {SSHA}arjnRIfyYQduvTQ7rdtVy6666mWIWtz3mj5Kdg==
mail: testymctesterson@example.edu
```

The ldapsearch tool is often supplied with the operating system, so if this command generates an **unrecognized option** error, check that you are running the *ldapsearch* provided with OpenDJ in the *bin* directory.

The logs for this little LDAP tree are located in */Users/username/OpenDJ/OpenDJ-2.4.5/ logs*. Run a tail on the access log while rerunning the `ldapsearch`, and you can confirm the connection:

tail -f logs/access

```
CONNECT conn=7 from=127.0.0.1:49994 to=127.0.0.1:1389 protocol=LDAP
BIND REQ conn=7 op=0 msgID=1 type=SIMPLE dn="uid=testy,
```

```
           ou=People,dc=example,dc=com"
BIND RES conn=7 op=0 msgID=1 result=0 authDN="uid=testy,
           ou=People,dc=example,dc=com" etime=1
SEARCH REQ conn=7 op=1 msgID=2 base="dc=example,dc=com"
         scope=wholeSubtree filter="(uid=testy)" attrs="ALL"
SEARCH RES conn=7 op=1 msgID=2 result=0 nentries=1 etime=1
UNBIND REQ conn=7 op=2 msgID=3
DISCONNECT conn=7 reason="Client Unbind"
```

In the same directory is the error log, named simply *error*. The goal is to not need that one.

Build and Install the OAE LDAP Modules

There are two parts to the LDAP Authentication setup: the connection service and the authentication service. The Connection service sets up, monitors, and breaks down connections to your ldap server. The Authentication service reacts to individual authentication events, drawing on ldap connections served up by the connection service.

The code for both modules is in the contrib subdirectory of the backend code downloaded and built back in Chapter 2. The nakamura contrib directory contains customization and integration code for authentication integration, database connectivity, and other extensions to the out-of-the-box configuration of OAE.

If you rebuilt the OAE code and started up the customized jar at the end of Chapter 4, shut that down and get back to working with the unbundled code by calling `tools/run_production.sh` from the *source/nakamura* directory. Seriously, make sure you have only one instance of OAE running. It's a sad, terrible day when you find you've been watching the logs on an OAE instance unattached to any port.

```
ps -ef | grep nakamura
```

should return just itself and one Java process.

LDAP Connection Service

Start by building the Connection Service bundle:

```
cd nakamura/contrib/ldap
mvn clean install
```

If you built the full system in Chapter 2 then this bundle should take under a minute to complete. The build will produce a bundle in the *nakamura/contrib/ldap/target* directory, with the name *org.sakaiproject.nakamura.ldap-1.2.0.jar*.

Before installing this first bundle, pop open a terminal and start watching the OAE log at *nakamura/sling/logs/error.log*:

```
tail -f sling/logs/error.log
```

To install the bundle, connect your browser to the administrative console at *http://localhost:8080/system/console*. Click the Bundles button to navigate to the bundles area (or just connect straight to *http://localhost:8080/system/console/bundles*).

Click the Install/Update... button towards the upper-right of the screen. In the Upload / Install Bundles dialog box leave the Start Bundle option unchecked, the Start Level value at the default of 20 and browse to your recently built org.sakaiproject.naka mura.ldap-1.2.jar bundle (see Figure 5-1). Click the Install or Update button.

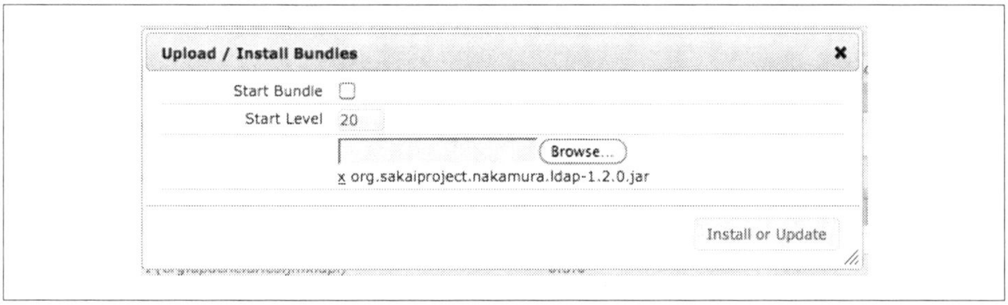

Figure 5-1. Install the LDAP bundle in the OSGi Bundles console

Sling won't immediately notify you that anything has changed. Refresh your browser and scroll down until you see the entry Sakai Nakamura :: LDAP Connection Bundle *org.sakaiproject.nakamura.ldap*. Entries are alphabetical, so it'll appear between the Sakai Nakamura :: JCR Bundle and Sakai Nakamura :: Locking Bundle bundles. The LDAP Connection bundle is listed with a status of Installed. Leave the status like that for now, as the bundle has to be configured before it can start up meaningfully.

Click the Configuration button at the top of the Sling web console (or just connect straight to *http://localhost:8080/system/console/configMgr*).

Scroll down to the Sakai Nakamura :: LDAP Pooling LDAP Connection Manager. Though the name is slightly different in the configuration view, this is the same bundle just installed. Click the "+" button to create a new LDAP connection pool. (See Figure 5-2.)

For quick demonstration purposes, set just the host and port values:

LDAP Host: **localhost**

LDAP Port: **1389**

Make sure that secure connection is unchecked, since there's no SSL certificate on this LDAP directory. Turn off Connection Pooling as well, so all activity is synchronized and log entries are created for each step in the LDAP process. Click the Save button, and refresh your browser in order to see that this has taken effect. There will be a new entry under Sakai Nakamura :: LDAP Pooling LDAP Connection Manager for org.sakai project.nakamura.ldap.PoolingLdapConnectionManager with a unique identifier appended. (See Figure 5-3.)

Figure 5-2. Configure the LDAP bundle

Flip back to the Bundles screen (*http://localhost:8080/system/console/bundles*). The status will likely have changed from Installed to Resolved while you were configuring the LDAP connection. Click the right arrow *play* button to start the Sakai Nakamura :: LDAP Connection Bundle. The bundle status will change from Resolved to Active.

In the *sling/logs/error.log* starting up the LDAP bundle will produce the following entries:

```
*INFO* [1567650495@qtp-2090567670-20] org.sakaiproject.nakamura.securityloader.Loader
Trying to Load security from bundle org.sakaiproject.nakamura.ldap.
*INFO* [1567650495@qtp-2090567670-20] org.sakaiproject.nakamura.ldap Service
```

```
[org.sakaiproject.nakamura.ldap.liveness.NativeLdapConnectionLivenessValidator,475]
ServiceEvent REGISTERED
*INFO* [1567650495@qtp-2090567670-20] org.sakaiproject.nakamura.ldap Service
[org.sakaiproject.nakamura.ldap.PoolingLdapConnectionManager.c8be33a6-fae1-46bc-
a71f-770dab5661aa,476] ServiceEvent REGISTERED
*INFO* [FelixDispatchQueue] org.sakaiproject.nakamura.ldap BundleEvent STARTED
```

Figure 5-3. LDAP bundle configuration appears as a fresh entry in the console

At this point the log is telling you that the configuration for the LDAP connection has valid syntax. It has not attempted to make an actual connection yet, so there won't be any new entries in the OpenDJ LDAP *logs/access* log. OAE will connect for the first time after you configure the ldap authentication service and attempt to authenticate via LDAP.

LDAP Authentication Service

Build the Authentication Service bundle:

```
cd nakamura/contrib/ldapauth
mvn clean install
```

The build will produce a bundle in the *nakamura/contrib/ldapauth/target* directory, with the name *org.sakaiproject.nakamura.auth.ldap-1.2.jar*. This bundle's name is distractingly similar to the connection bundle. The authentication service bundle is named with *nakamura.auth.ldap*, where the connection service is just *nakamura.ldap*.

Back in your browser click the Sling web console `Bundles` button to navigate to the bundles area, if you're not already there.

Click the `Install/Update…` button towards the upper-right of the screen. Again, leave the `Start Bundle` option unchecked, the `Start Level` value at the default of 20 and browse to the newly built `org.sakaiproject.nakamura.auth.ldap-1.2.jar` bundle from the *ldapauth/target* directory (see Figure 5-4). Click the `Install or Update` button.

Upload / Install Bundles		✕
Start Bundle	☐	
Start Level	20	
	(Browse…)	
	x org.sakaiproject.nakamura.auth.ldap-1.2.0.jar	
		Install or Update

Figure 5-4. Install the LDAP Auth bundle in the OSGi Bundles console

Refresh your browser and scroll down until you see the entry Sakai Nakamura :: LDAP Authentication Bundle. This will appear just above the Sakai Nakamura :: LDAP Connection Bundle. The Authentication bundle will be shown with a status of Installed. Again, hold off on making the bundle active until after it's configured.

Click the Configuration button. Scroll down and you'll find two configuration elements have been introduced by the LDAP Authentication service: Sakai Nakamura :: LDAP Authentication Plugin and Sakai Nakamura :: LDAP Login Module Plugin.

Start by configuring the Authentication Plugin. Where the Connection service permits multiple instances, the Authentication Plugin always has only one, so it is presented in the Configuration manager with a pencil button instead of a "+" button. Click the pencil button to open up the configuration dialog (see Figure 5-5). Enter the following values to connect to your demonstration LDAP system:

Base DN: **ou=People,dc=example,dc=com**

User Filter: **uid={}**

Authorization Filter: set to blank, we'll start off without an authorization filter.

Create account for user?: Leave checked

Properties from LDAP: **{ givenName:firstName, sn:lastName, mail:email }**

Click Save.

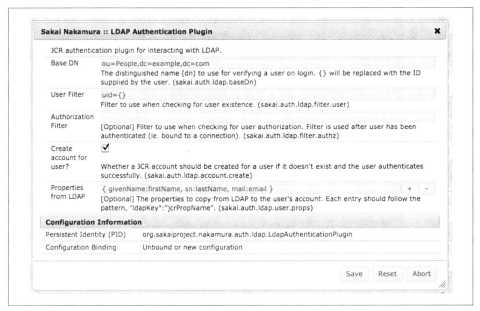

Figure 5-5. Configure the LDAP Auth bundle

Flip back to the Bundles screen (*http://localhost:8080/system/console/bundles*). The status will likely have changed from Installed to Resolved while you were configuring the LDAP connection. Click the right arrow *play* button to start the Sakai Nakamura :: LDAP Authentication bundle. The bundle status will change from Resolved to Active.

In the *sling/logs/error.log* the following log entries are written as the bundle starts up:

```
*INFO* [1873647547@qtp-2090567670-40] org.sakaiproject.nakamura.securityloader.Loader
Trying to load security from bundle org.sakaiproject.nakamura.auth.ldap.
*INFO* [1873647547@qtp-2090567670-40] org.sakaiproject.nakamura.auth.ldap Service
[org.sakaiproject.nakamura.auth.ldap.LdapAuthenticationPlugin,479] ServiceEvent
REGISTERED
*INFO* [1873647547@qtp-2090567670-40] org.sakaiproject.nakamura.auth.ldap Service
[org.sakaiproject.nakamura.auth.ldap.LdapLoginModulePlugin,480] ServiceEvent
REGISTERED
*INFO* [FelixDispatchQueue] org.sakaiproject.nakamura.auth.ldap BundleEvent STARTED
```

Again, no actual LDAP connection has been attempted, so no entries appear in the LDAP *access* log.

We're now ready to test—and get an actual LDAP connection at last.

Quit your browser completely, or change over to a different web browser. When you log in to the Sling console, the browser caches the admin credentials, making it impossible to log out without quitting the browser (see "A Quick Trick for Checking Permissions" on page 35).

Connect your browser to *http://localhost:8080* and sign in with the credentials **testy** and **ldap_password**, as created by importing the ldif file in "Set Up a Mini LDAP Instance" on page 65. If your LDAP setup is functioning correctly, you'll land on Testy McTesterson's dashboard in OAE.

Click down to the My profile Basic Information section though, and you'll see there's a problem. There's no profile information, and no way to provide any. An attempt to access Mr. McTesterson's public profile page at *http://localhost:8080/~testy* will generate a *404 Page not found* error. While the Titanic 404 error page is quite nice, it's definitely not the desired behavior. For more on what it takes to implement automatic user provisioning, see the sidebar "Advanced Topics: Cracking Open the LDAP Authentication Plug-in" on page 84.

In large schools and universities, it's common to do some preconfiguration on users' accounts, provisioning the account before the users' first access to the system, a bit like making up the guest room because you know friends are due to arrive. To implement this version of events, first modify the LDAP Authentication Configuration so as to not create the users' account on first login.

In the Configuration section of the administrative console at *http://localhost:8080/system/console/configMgr*, click the pencil button to modify the configuration for Sakai Nakamura :: LDAP Authentication Plugin. Clear the checkbox next to Create account for user? and click the Save button. The change in configuration is adopted without having to restart the bundle or the system.

To show this, quit and restart the browser, to clear out the admin credentials. Attempt to login with the username paul and password ldap_password. In the web browser, it will look like you don't know your password. Under the covers in the error log though, it shows the actual state of affairs:

```
*INFO* [1023596284@qtp-1184762925-22]
org.sakaiproject.nakamura.auth.ldap.LdapAuthenticationPlugin User [uid=paul]
authenticated with LDAP in 86ms
*INFO* [1023596284@qtp-1184762925-22]
org.apache.sling.auth.core.impl.SlingAuthenticator handleLoginFailure:
Unable to authenticate null: Workspace access denied
```

The authentication check for Paul succeeded, but then he was blocked from getting to the dashboard. This is because the dashboard doesn't exist and you've revoked OAE's permission to create one. You can see that no user account was created by navigating in your web browser to Explore→People (*http://localhost:8080/search#l=people*). The damaged account for Testy shows up, but there is no listing for Paul.

To create Paul's account use a curl script: create a shell script with the name *Create-Paul.sh* and contents (keep the argument after -d in double quotes on one line):

```
#!/bin/sh

(curl -d "pwd=local_password&pwdConfirm=local_password&firstName=Paul&lastName=Erdos&
:name=paul&:sakai:profile-import={\"basic\": {\"elements\": {\"firstName\":
{\"value\": \"Paul\"}, \"lastName\": {\"value\": \"Erdos\"}, \"email\": {\"value\":
\"erdos@example.edu\"}, \"college\": {\"value\": \"Institute for Advanced Study
\"}}}}" \
--referer http://localhost:8080/dev/test.html \
http://admin:admin@localhost:8080/system/userManager/user.create.html \
>/dev/null 2>/dev/null \
        && echo Created paul ) \
        || echo ERROR creating paul
```

Make the script executable and call it from the command line:

chmod +x CreatePaul.sh

./CreatePaul.sh

```
Created paul
```

Now, login at *http://localhost:8080* with the username paul and password ldap_pass word. This time Paul can log in. Click on his My profile Basic Information section (see Figure 5-6). The profile is properly populated, with the values from the CreatePaul.sh script, not with the LDAP values. Where the LDAP entry has an email address of paul@example.edu, our curl-created account shows the email address as erdos@example.edu.

Figure 5-6. Paul's Preconfigured Profile

OAE and the Delete Function

This is probably a good time to mention one of the more unexpected design choices regarding the user delete function. There isn't one. User login credentials can be revoked. User profiles can be hidden from the view of everyone but the system administrators. User accounts can't be destroyed, however.

OAE assumes a high level of collaboration among its participants. Everyone who contributes material, or modifies it, or comments on it, becomes in that act a part of the community memory. Removing an account would require removal or reconceptualization of all that memory.

There may be users who need to access OAE, but who aren't ever going to be in your LDAP server. For example, the `admin` user is established by default to manage the system console of OAE. Rather than require that the LDAP authority get involved for every account, OAE provides a filter function, which checks designated accounts only against the local set of credentials.

Click over to the Configuration screen in the console at *http://localhost:8080/system/ console/configMgr*. Scroll down to the `Sakai Nakamura :: LDAP Login Module Plugin`. This is the second configuration panel installed with the LDAP Authentication bundle. It's separated out from the general configuration panel because there are a limited number of instances in which you want to use the Login Module, and it uses regular expressions for its filter language. Cue the chestnut from Jamie Zawinski: "Some people, when confronted with a problem, think 'I know, I'll use regular expressions.' Now they have two problems." To exercise it, modify the `Username Filter` to replace `^admin$` with `^(admin|paul)$`. This has the effect of excluding precisely two usernames from LDAP authentication: the `admin` user and `paul`. Click the `Save` button, quit, and restart your browser to clear the admin credentials. (Isn't it time you got used to using two separate browser products to test? See "A Quick Trick for Checking Permissions" on page 35.) If you're connected as `paul`, log out. Now when you log back in as `paul`, using the password `ldap_password` (as set in LDAP by the ldif file) will fail, but using the password `local_password` (as set by the `curl` command in the `Create Paul.sh` script) will succeed. To see that LDAP continues to be used for everyone else, login in as `testy` with the password `ldap_password`.

Getting Out of Trouble

Be very, very careful with your LDAP Login Module Plug-in Username Filter. You can lock yourself out as the admin by accidentally excluding the admin user from the Username Filter. You'll know you've done this if every time you try to access the console you are confronted with the authentication challenge for the OSGi Management Console, and credentials that worked before you modified the `Username Filter` work no more.

If you get yourself into trouble, there are two ways out: wipe out your system and restart with a clean set up or manually modify the *LdapLoginModulePlugin.config* file. Wiping the system should be reserved for when you're truly out of hope. See "Starting Clean" on page 120 for instructions on the nuclear option.

The `LdapLoginModulePlugin.config` file is located within your *nakamura* directory, in the subdirectory *nakamura/sling/config/org/sakaiproject/nakamura/auth/ldap*. Modify the user filter property to the simplest admin permission, leaving the other parameters in this file as they are:

```
sakai.login.ldap.user.filter="^admin$"
```

Save the *.config* file. In order to force OAE to reload the config, stop and restart the whole system.

Consider one of the fine O'Reilly titles on Regular Expressions (*http://search.oreilly .com/?q=regular+expressions&x=0&y=0*) while you wait for the system to restart and let you back in.

Troubleshooting LDAP Configuration Settings

If you can't log in once LDAP is hooked up, take a look at the error log at *sling/logs/ error.log*. The error of interest is generated at the moment of attempting log in.

`Unable to authenticate null: LoginModule ignored Credentials`

This may indicate the `Sakai Nakamura :: LDAP Authentication Bundle` has been configured, but hasn't been started. Make sure the status for the LDAP Authentication Bundle is `Active`.

`java.lang.IllegalArgumentException:Can't find user`

The search string looks right, but OAE can't find the user often means that the base DN and user string have gotten flipped.

`com.novell.ldap.LDAPException:No Such Object`

This error tracks with a bad base DN value, for example, entering uid={},ou=People,dc=example,dc=com instead of just dc=example,dc=com.

`java.lang.ArrayIndexOutOfBoundsException: 0`

In the LDAP Authentication configuration, even if you disable the setting for `Create account for user?` the system still expects a value for `Properties from LDAP`. The system expects a value in this field despite the field clearly being labeled *Optional*. Someday, it will be different.

`Not all dependencies satisified, cannot activate [FelixDispatchQueue]`

The LDAP Authentication bundle has been started, but without an associated LDAP Connection bundle running. Attempting to log in via the web interface will fail, even with correct credentials. Start the LDAP Connection bundle, wait about a minute, and try again.

`com.novell.ldap.LDAPLocalException:Filter Error`

The LDAP Authentication bundle configuration has something unexpected in the Authorization filter field. Set the Authorization filter to an empty value, then start to build the filter up from scratch again. Check with your LDAP administrator to make sure something hasn't changed.

Additional useful information will be in the LDAP log. Look for whether or not a connection has been attempted, and if attempted any indicator on why the connection or the lookup failed.

Choose Your Configuration (and Configure It)

In practice, you'll receive your LDAP configuration settings from on high (or from a system admin, which is approximately the same). If you present your LDAP administrator with the list of parameters, you'll probably get a list of answers back without having to have any conversation beyond amiable grunts.

If you find yourself in the extraordinary position of jointly negotiating the right decisions with your LDAP administrator, here's a wayfinding guide.

LDAP Host

This is your most straightforward setting. There's only one name for your LDAP host. It should be in the standard domain name format, and should not have any protocol information in front of it, so no `ldap://` or `ldaps://` prefix.

LDAP Host: *yourldapserver.example.edu*

SSLing the Connection

You want to communicate from OAE to your university LDAP over SSL. You just do. Don't think about it. Don't argue about it. Just admit that in production you want to run over SSL.

In order to do so, your LDAP Administrator will have to set up ldaps on the institutional LDAP system. If the SSL configuration uses a proper certificate issued by a recognized certificate authority (CA) then your security setup will be fairly straightforward. In the `Sakai Nakamura :: LDAP Pooling LDAP Connection Manager`:

Secure Connection: *checked*

LDAP Port: **636**.

Unencrypted LDAP traffic usually travels on **389**; SSL LDAP travels on **636**. If your LDAP admin has changed this from the default, they will tell you. (Probably, if you ask nicely.)

Often LDAP isn't worth the cost or annoyance of purchasing a proper certificate from a certificate authority. Unlike a public facing https service, all the consumers of the ldaps service are members of your IT community. If the institutional LDAP configuration uses a self-signed certificate for ldaps service, then you'll need to obtain a copy of the keystore that corresponds to the self-signed certificate. Your LDAP admin will provide you with the keystore and associated password. Keystores are generally suffixed .jks for Java KeyStore. Alternatively you may be provided with a plain text certificate, which you'll need to import into a keystore on your OAE server. In that case you'll be selecting the password for your keystore at the time you import the certificate. The Internet is awash in good, up-to-date tutorials on how to set up a keystore. One good one is the original Java tutorial, now at Oracle: *http://docs.oracle.com/javase/tuto rial/security/toolsign/rstep2.html*.

If you're working with a self-signed certificate, then you'll need to set four parameters in the `Sakai Nakamura :: LDAP Pooling LDAP Connection Manager`:

Secure Connection: *checked*

LDAP Port: *636*

Keystore Location: */directoryname/keystorename.jks*

Keystore password: *your keystore password*

If no amount of rational debate can bring your LDAP admins to SSL the LDAP traffic, then you just need the two settings in Sakai Nakamura :: LDAP Pooling LDAP Connection Manager:

Secure Connection: *not checked*

LDAP Port: **389**

Bind User

The preferred model for setting up LDAP authentication is to permit individual users the smallest range of possible permissions on the LDAP tree and to provide authenticating applications with a bind user account which has greater visibility. The little OpenDJ server set up permitted any user to read down the hash of every user's password. That is really bad form, and should never be permitted in real life.

You'll need to ask your LDAP admin to set up an authorized bind user for you. Usually there's a standard institutional process for requesting these, which might involve filling out paperwork and bringing caffeinated beverages to the LDAP admin's desk every day for a week. The bind user will often appear in a different area of the LDAP tree, so if your user accounts are in "ou=People,dc=example,dc=com" then your bind user might be in "ou=Special People,dc=example,dc=com." To set up a bind user, set the bind DN and password values in the Sakai Nakamura :: LDAP Pooling LDAP Connection Manager configuration. The bind DN in this instance includes both the username value and the full DN for locating the bind user.

User DN: **uid=bindusername,ou=Special People,dc=example,dc=com**

Password: **bind_user_password**

Another way of providing the bind credentials is to link them to the operating system user running your Sakai OAE system. In order to function, LDAPI must be enabled, and appropriate privileges must be granted to an LDAP user that matches the operating system user. Once configured, this is enabled with the **autobind** checkbox in the Sakai Nakamura :: LDAP Pooling LDAP Connection Manager configuration. Some consider LDAPI/autobind configurations to be insecure, so have some serious conversations with experts before pursuing this path.

Performance Considerations

Three parameters can be used to tune the LDAP connectivity. In production, connection pooling should definitely be turned on. The right size for the maximum number of connections in the pool will depend on the actual usage characteristics of your system. On the one hand, a large maximum number will reduce the frequency with which authentication attempts have to block and wait for a free connection. On the other, keeping a large number of idle connections open can exhaust resources unneccesarily. The default of 10 is a good starting point for maximum connections in the pool. The connection timeout controls two events: how long an individual connection waits for a response from the LDAP server and how long an authentication attempt waits for a connection from the pool. If the timeout's not set, the system will wait forever for a connection, probably not an ideal situation. The default of 5000 milliseconds is a good starting point.

Connection Timeout: **5000**

Connection Pooling: **checked**

Max Connections in Pool: **10**

Authorization

Authorization often gets blended with authentication. It's worth pausing to think about them as separate events for a moment. Authentication is about whether you are who you say you are. Authorization is whether you have permission to do anything, now that we know who you are.

Authorization happens at a couple of levels in OAE. On the really granular level, the application itself controls authorization: whether you've shared specific items with the world, a group, an individual, with all logged in users, or kept it private. Instructors can pull together a course site, and decide which items to share with their students and which to share with their teaching assistants. Privacy and publication are at the heart of OAE's functionality.

The most common way Internet systems ask people to prove who they are is with a username-password combination. If you know the secret password that corresponds to your username, then that's sufficient to prove that you are who you say you are. If George Washington had an account on our OAE install, and he turned up and knew the right password, then the system would let him in.

Authorization is permitting you access based on who you are. If George turned up, and was believably George, we still wouldn't let him walk into the Oval Office. There are multiple levels of authorization in Sakai OAE. The deepest and most detailed authorizations are at the heart of what makes OAE useful. Sharing or protecting.

The LDAP bundles can control the level of authorization associated with "logged in users." There are four variations on how this can be implemented. The first two rely on OAE automatically creating a user account the first time the person logs in. The hooks for creating users on authentication are in OAE, but the implementation is on a school-by-school basis.

- Everyone with valid LDAP credentials can access Sakai OAE:

  Authorization Filter: **leave blank**

  Create account for user?: **checked**

- Limit access to a subset of LDAP users:

  Set an entitlement value in LDAP, identifying individuals who are permitted to login to OAE. For example LDAP records can include an *eduPersonEntitlement* like `urn:mace:`*example:com*`:entl:lib:oae`. If a user has the entitlement, they are permitted through to OAE; if not, they are blocked from logging in, even if they enter their correct password. Enter the entitlement and its valid value in the `Authorization Filter` field in `Sakai Nakamura :: LDAP Authentication Plugin`.

  `Authorization Filter:` **`eduPersonEntitlement=urn:mace:`*`example:com`*`:entl:lib:`**
  `oae`

  `Create account for user?:` **`checked`**

- Limit access to prepopulated user accounts:

  `Authorization Filter`: can be blank, or can be an LDAP entitlement if you want to get all belt and suspenders on authorization control.

  `Create account for user?:` **`unchecked`**

  To precreate accounts, use a set of scripts similar to the *CreatePaul.sh* script.

The Sakai OAE error.log will show which attempts failed on authentication and which on the various kinds of authorization. The person logging in will get the same message in all cases: `Invalid username or password`.

RESTful Account Creation

Simple user accounts can be preprovisioned at the command line via the REST interface at `system/userManager/user.create.html`. The curl tool is handy for interacting over HTTP with the REST APIs (see more about curl at "Set Up Curl" on page 95), but a curl line can be a bit much for a human to read. For example, the following `curl` command when executed all on one line creates an account with the username phyllis:

```
        curl -d "pwd=local_password&pwdConfirm=local_password&firstName=Phyllis
&lastName=Chinn&:name=phyllis&:sakai:profile-import={\"basic\":
{\"elements\":{\"firstName\": {\"value\": \"Phyllis\"},\"lastName\":
{\"value\": \"Chinn\"}, \"email\": {\"value\":\"phyllis@example.edu\"},
\"college\": {\"value\": \"Humboldt State University\"}}}}" \
--referer http://localhost:8080/dev/test.html
http://admin:admin@localhost:8080/system/userManager/user.create.html
```

Broken into its constituent parts, the API call looks like this:

```
curl -d
    "pwd=local_password
    &pwdConfirm=local_password
    &firstName=Phyllis
    &lastName=Chinn
    &:name=phyllis
    &:sakai:profile-import=
```

```
      {\"basic\":
        {\"elements\":
          {\"firstName\":
              {\"value\": \"Phyllis\"},
          \"lastName\":
              {\"value\": \"Chinn\"},
          \"email\":
              {\"value\": \"phyllis@example.edu\"},
          \"college\":
              {\"value\": \"Humboldt State University\"}
          }
        }
      }"
--referer http://localhost:8080/dev/test.html
http://admin:admin@localhost:8080/system/userManager/user.create.html
```

The first five elements set up the internal values for the Sakai OAE account: password, first name, last name, and username. The next part, `:sakai:profile-import,` corresponds to the About Me information in a person's profile. A referer value must be provided, though from the command line on the application server it is sufficient to send a dummy value like `dev/test.html`. The very last line authenticates as the administrative user and issues the API call to `user.create.html`.

The results come back as a fully formed HTTP response, which again, can be a bit much for a human to read. To create many accounts, wrap the `curl` commands in a shell script, similar to the `CreatePaul.sh` one created earlier in this chapter, which captures the response codes instead of attempting to parse the HTTP response.

Advanced Topics: Cracking Open the LDAP Authentication Plug-in

Automated LDAP account provisioning fell victim at some point to improvements in profile handling. The frontend of Sakai OAE has made it easy to extend and refine the profile properties for a given school, and to establish which are required, optional, which must be public and which properties can be taken private by the account owner. The backend has been factored to be highly tolerant of these customizations, delivering profile data smoothly without needing to know *a priori* what it is. The piece left behind was account provisioning within the LDAP Authentication bundle, which needs to know what a profile looks like in order to provision it.

Account provisioning, when configured to execute, is done by the *LdapAuthenticationPlugin* class, within the *GetJcrUser* method:

```
private Authorizable getJcrUser(Session session, String userId) throws Exception {
    AuthorizableManager am = session.getAuthorizableManager();
    Authorizable auth = am.findAuthorizable(userId);
    if (auth == null && createAccount) {
        String password = RandomStringUtils.random(8);
        boolean created = am.createUser(userId, userId, password, null);
```

```
        if (created) {
            auth = am.findAuthorizable(userId);
            authorizablePostProcessService.process(auth, session,
              ModificationType.CREATE, null);
        }
        else {
            throw new Exception("Unable to create User for " + userId);
        }
    }
  return auth;
  }
```

The account is initially created by the call to *AuthorizableManager.createUser()*. If the account creation is succesful, then the associated *Authorizable* is retrieved and its profile properties are initialized by the call to the *authorizablePostProcessService.process* method. Note the *modificationType.CREATE* flag in the third position. The last parameter in the process call, set to *null* in this example, is the actual property set for the user's profile. This parameter is expected to be a Map<String, Object[]> and the contents must match the required profile fields set in the frontend code.

University of California, Berkeley has published their automated account provisioning classes at *http://github.com/ets-berkeley-edu/myberkeley* in the *provision* area. Though their authentication service links to the CAS single sign-on infrastructure, the *CalOaeAuthorizableService* class offers a good example of how to provision automatically against a locally defined profile.

Removing the Self-Service Functions

Once OAE is integrated to central authentication, you don't want people to go around willy-nilly creating accounts they can't access. Here's the three step process for thoroughly removing self-registration and password resetting from the system.

These changes involve modifying the *config.js* file, so you'll need to modify the Apache Sling Filesystem Resource Provider as in "Configure OAE for CSS, Property, and JavaScript Changes" on page 41. Only the */dev* filesystem resource needs to be set up for disabling account creation and password resetting.

To turn off access to the Sign Up functions, in *dev/configuration/config.js* (after making a safe copy, of course) modify the allowInternalAccountCreation value, setting it to false:

```
        "allowInternalAccountCreation": false,
```

Empty your browser cache, and refresh the browser. The Sign Up link is removed from the top-left navigation, and no longer appears in the Sign In drop-down. Accessing the registration page at *http://localhost:8080/register* just redirects the browser back to the dashboard (see Figure 5-7).

Figure 5-7. Sign Up link removed from the Sign In area

To turn off access to the password reset function in the `My Account` area, modify the `allowPasswordChange` value in *config.js*, setting it to false:

```
allowPasswordChange: false,
```

Empty your browser cache and again refresh the browser. Log in as Paul or another test user, if you're not already. From the name menu on the upper-right, select `My account`. The `My account` dialog now offers only the `Preferences` and `Privacy settings` tabs (see Figure 5-8). The `Password` tab is gone.

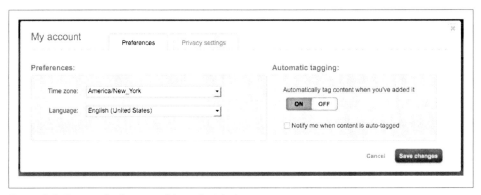

Figure 5-8. Password tab removed from the My Account area

There's one more step for disabling self-registration. The *allowInternalAccountCreation* setting removes account creation from the frontend of OAE, but it might be possible for a knowledgeable person to access the backend user account creation process[1]. To disable the backend service as well, engage in a bit of OSGi magic. Create a directory named *load* in your *nakamura* directory, as a sibling to the *sling* directory that was created there the first time you started up OAE. In this new *nakamura/load* directory, create an empty file with the name *org.sakaiproject.nakamura.user.lite.servlet.LiteCreateSakaiUserServlet.cfg*:

```
cd /nakamura/load/
```

---

1. Hacking is left as an exercise for the reader.

```
touch \
org.sakaiproject.nakamura.user.lite.servlet.LiteCreateSakaiUserServlet.cfg
```

To this, add a single parameter, disabling the self registration service on the backend:

```
echo 'self.registration.enabled=false' >> \
org.sakaiproject.nakamura.user.lite.servlet.LiteCreateSakaiUserServlet.cfg
```

Why this janky method? The *load* directory is automagically read and maintained by the Felix File Install management agent, a part of the OSGi container. If you edit the *.cfg* file in an interactive manner you may get a file lock error to the effect of:

```
WARNING: The file has been changed since reading it!!!
Do you really want to write to it (y/n)?:
```

To make sure the change took effect head back to the system console at *http://localhost: 8080/system/console*. Click the Component button. Up until now, you've been working with Sakai OAE *bundles* and their associated *configurations*. OAE OSGi *components* don't necessarily have editable configurations associated with them. Creating a *.cfg* file in the *load* directory allows you to gain access to component configuration settings. On the Components console scroll down to org.sakaiproject.nakamura.user.lite.serv let.LiteCreateSakaiUserServlet. Click on this listing to display the details for the LiteCreateSakaiUserServlet. Under the Properties section, the value for self.regis tration.enabled is now false.

Re-enabling self registration, should you need to, can be done interactively in the Components console. Once a configuration file is associated with a component, a little Configure button with a wrench icon on it turns up next to the component listing. Click the wrench button and modify the value of self.registration.enabled to true, then save. This has the effect of updating two files on disk: one the original configuration file you created in the *load* directory, and the other a *.config* suffixed equivalent in the *sling/config* directory structure (see "Where, Oh, Where Has My CFG Gone? Oh, Where, Oh Where Could It Be?" on page 111).

CHAPTER 6

Building On

Widgets provide a way to extend and customize the core functionality of Sakai OAE. Some widgets are designed to appear on individual's dashboards, providing access to popular content or to information from beyond OAE. Other widgets are for inclusion in groups, courses, and projects, or on an individual page. Some special widgets are embedded within the framework, like the welcome widget modified in "Change the Landing Page" on page 60.

A widget library collects contributions from schools, organizations, and individuals. It's still a little sparse, but that's kind of the point. The OAE project is building the infrastructure. Widgets are all the little corners of functionality that the core team hasn't thought of. Let's look at three widgets to give you a flavor.

To install a widget first unzip, build, and configure the frontend OAE code as for Skinning in Chapter 4. Widget installation requires only customizations to the */devwidgets* space, so if the skin is unchanging there's no need to configure a File System Resource for */dev*, only one for */devwidgets*.

A Very Simple Dashboard Widget: JISC Content Browser

The JISC is a UK organization supporting the use of digitial technology in higher education. The JISC Content browser widget pulls a JISC resident widget into the OAE environment, making it easy to discover content available through the JISC. Almost no code is executed within the OAE environment.

Connect to the Widget Library at *http://oae-widgets.sakaiproject.org* and enter `jisc` in the search box. Click the `Download` button to retrieve the JISC Content widget code, *jisccontent.zip*. Unzip the code into the `sakai-ux/devwidgets` directory.

Once the widget is deployed to the devwidgets directory, it's immediately available in OAE.

Login in at *http://locahost:8080*. The JISC Content widget looks best in a two-column layout, so start by clicking the `Edit Layout` button and selecting the two column layout option.

To add the JISC Content widget, click the `Add Widget` button. Next to the JISC content entry, click the `Add` button and close the `Add widgets` box. The JISC Content widget is added at the bottom of the lefthand column on the dashboard (see Figure 6-1). The widget provides a quick view of the content collection. Clicking on a collection opens the JISC Content website. The widget is not terribly useful in North America since access to the content is limited to the UK.

Figure 6-1. A very simple dashboard widget (bottom left)

Cracking open the code gives a nice glimpse at a very simple widget. The *jisccontent.html* file contains an iframe, which adopts the JISC content widget directly from *jisc-content.ac.uk*. That's all it takes.

```
<!-- CSS -->
<link rel="stylesheet" type="text/css" href="/devwidgets/jisccontent/css/
jisccontent.css" />

<div class="jisccontent_widget">
    <div class="jisccontent_widget_content">
        <iframe width="100%" height="300" frameborder="0"
                title="__MSG__JISC_CONTENT__"
```

```
                    src="http://www.jisc-content.ac.uk/widget"></iframe>
        </div>
    </div>
```

The other files in the *jisccontent* directory are the infrastructure that make up the widget: a configuration *.json* file, a CSS file, and the localization *.properties* file. The `__MSG__JISC_CONTENT__` parameter in the HTML is replaced by the `JISC_CONTENT` value in the *.properties* file for the widget. To translate and localize a widget, language specific properties files can be included directly with the widget.

A Group Widget: Simplified Comments

The comments wall widget is a simplified version of the default Comment Stream widget. This widget is designed for inclusion in the navigation menu of a group, course, or research project, which are referred to by the collective noun `world` in the OAE technical community. From the OAE widget library, download the `Comments Wall` widget. Unzip the *commentswall.zip* widget code into the *sakai-ux/devwidgets* directory.

To add the comment stream widget, as a group manager click the `Add+` button on the lefthand navigation of the group. In the Add dialog box, select `Widgets` at the bottom of the list of materials available to add and select `Comments wall` from the `Select a widget` drop-down list (see Figure 6-2). Enter a name, which will appear on the left navigation and click the `Done, add` button. Enter a few comments to see the layout of this version of a comment widget. This comments widget is not hugely different from the Comment Stream widget provided with OAE by default. Every institution is different, and one comment style may well be vastly preferred over the other within a local culture.

Taking a look in the *commentswall* directory in the *devwidgets* space, this widget includes a *javascript* directory. The *commentswall.js* file has the logic for this widget, writing and retrieving comment text from OAE storage. In addition the widget relies on the same kind of *.html*, *.css*, *config.json*, and *properties* bundle infrastructure as the JISC Content widget.

A Complex Widget: Walking Time Map

University of California, Berkeley has built a widget to provide estimated times to walk between buildings on their campus. Recognizing that this could be useful to other schools, the programmers generalized it and submitted it to the OAE Widget Library. To install it on your OAE, download the `WalkTime` widget from the Library and unzip it to the *devwidgets* directory. This widget resides on the dashboard. Add it and check out some standard distances on their campus.

Figure 6-2. Adding Comments Wall to the left navigation of a group

To modify the widget to show locations for your environment, modify the *map_coordinates.xml* file. For example, in New York City there are a number of great libraries within what New Yorkers consider walking distance:

```xml
<?xml version="1.0"?>
<Locations>
<Location>
  <Name>Bobst Library, NYU</Name>
  <Lat>40.729513</Lat>
  <Lon>-73.997145</Lon>
</Location>
<Location>
  <Name>Butler Library, Columbia</Name>
  <Lat>40.806454</Lat>
  <Lon>-73.963148</Lon>
</Location>
<Location>
  <Name>New York Public Library, Main Branch</Name>
  <Lat>40.753174</Lat>
  <Lon>-73.981957</Lon>
</Location>
<Location>
  <Name>Brooklyn Public Library</Name>
  <Lat>40.672273</Lat>
  <Lon>-73.968165</Lon>
</Location>
</Locations>
```

There's one more change to make, this one in *javascript/walktime.js*, to modify the `defaultCoords` value to match a starting point in the `map_coordinates.xml` file:

```
// New default position is NYPL Main Branch
var defaultCoords = [40.753174,-73.981957,40.753174,-73.981957];
```

Refresh the widget, and you'll have directions for wandering the fair city of New York as in Figure 6-3. If you like this widget and want to deploy it for your school, NASA provides a great little latitude/longitude lookup tool at *http://mynasadata.larc.nasa.gov/ LatLon.html*.

Figure 6-3. The walking time widget as it appears to the user

The Widget SDK

Widget development can be very straightforward or remarkably complicated. Anything that can be done in JavaScript can be wrapped up and shared as a widget. On the OAE Widget Library there's a full SDK site at *http://oae-widgets.sakaiproject.org/sdk*, including examples, style guides, and instructions on how to contribute widgets back to the community.

CHAPTER 7

Scaling Up

Now, you're ready for production. This chapter covers the wide variety of integration and finalization choices for OAE in production.

The Basics

There are a handful of things that must be set before opening OAE up for people to use. The admin password must be changed, outgoing email configured, start and stop scripts established, and logs put under rotation. OAE provides RESTful web services for most functions, so you can use curl as a command-line administrative interface.

Set Up Curl

Curl is a simple command line tool for accessing URLs. It can handle http, https, ftp as well as many other common transfer protocols. Both curl and the library libcurl are freely available open source software. Precompiled binaries for some 60 platforms are available at *http://curl.haxx.se/download.html*, but chances are it is already on your system. Anything in the 7 family will be just fine. If you have a curl version 6 on your machine, consider donating it to the American Computing Museum:

`curl —version`

```
curl 7.16.4 (i386-apple-darwin9.0) libcurl/7.16.4 OpenSSL/0.9.7l zlib/1.2.3
```

A couple of particularly useful parameters are:

`--referer`

OAE requires that every http request include the referring page that originated the request. Requiring a referrer reduces OAE's exposure to simple cross-site request forgery attacks. You'll notice though that referrer data can easily be passed in. You'll also notice that one stray misspelling can take unstoppable root in a software system.

-O

The binary retrieval examples in "Binary Install" on page 8 show the use of the -O parameter to name the local file the same as the remote one. Curl is a transfer tool; the data coming in is just a stream of bytes from curl's perspective. The -O parameter obviates the need to explicitly redirect the stream (e.g., **curl -O http://example.edu/index.html** instead of **curl http://example.edu/index.html > index.html**).

-F

Curl can emulate the submission of a web form. The -F parameter is followed by a name and value pair that corresponds to a filled-in field on the form. For every field on a given form, the -F parameter repeats with the appropriate name and value pair. If the name or value has one of the special characters @ or < in it, the parameter --form-string can be used to ignore those characters.

-u

Curl logs in transparently as the designated user with the given password. Note that the password passes in the clear. The administrator credentials should be passed only on the local system. It should never go across an open network. As you accumulate curl-based scripts, be mindful of how you store and secure credentials passed to OAE in REST oriented administrative tasks.

-s -o /dev/null

The -s parameter sets silent mode, which prevents curl from displaying error messages or progress bars. The -o parameter, similar to the -O parameter above, sets the name of the output file, in this case, a redirect to the */dev/null* pseudofile. This can be useful in scripts, where you want to capture the HTTP response code, but not any of the other output.

Change the Admin Password

Sakai OAE installs with the admin password set to admin—not exactly a hard password to guess, particularly now that it's in print. The admin user is the empowered user both for OAE and for the underlying Felix OSGi container.

There is a Sling REST call specifically for changing the admin password. The current password is provided twice: once in the -u parameter to connect and once as the oldPwd parameter. Call it with curl:

```
curl -uadmin:admin -FoldPwd=admin -FnewPwd=new_password \
-FnewPwdConfirm=new_password --referer http://localhost:8080/dev/test.html \
http://localhost:8080/system/userManager/user/admin.changePassword.html
```

A slightly nicer shell script to accomplish the same:

```
#!/bin/sh
ADMIN_PWD='admin'
NEW_PWD='new_password'
```

```
# Next bit needs to be all on one line
HTTP_RETURN=`curl  -s -o /dev/null -w '%{http_code}' -u "admin:${ADMIN_PWD}"
-F"oldPwd={ADMIN_PWD}" -F"newPwd=${NEW_PWD}" -F"newPwdConfirm=${NEW_PWD}"
--referer http://localhost:8080/dev/test.html
http://localhost:8080/system/userManager/user/admin.changePassword.html`

if [[ $HTTP_RETURN == 200 ]]; then
  echo "Admin password changed to '"$NEW_PWD"'"
elif [[ $HTTP_RETURN == 401 ]]; then
  echo "Admin password not changed. Password provided is probably not correct."
else
  echo "Unhandled http response" $HTTP_RETURN
fi
```

Once you've changed the password, you'll need to use the new value for all administrative curl calls and for logging into the system console.

Outgoing Email

Sakai OAE can send email to people when something interesting happens in the system, like an invitation to connect with someone or a new message in the inbox. To configure the email-out system, connect to the system console, and click the Configuration button (*http://localhost:8080/system/console/configMgr*).

The configuration parameters for outgoing email are in org.sakaiproject.naka mura.email.outgoing.LiteOutgoingEmailMessageListener.name. Click the pencil icon to modify the settings. By default email messages appear to come from the email address no-reply@example.com, which one hopes people will not attempt to reply to. Modify the Reply-As Address and Reply-As Name to reflect your university standard.

sakai.email.replyAsAddress: *support@my.edu*

sakai.email.replyAsName: *Myedu Community Manager*

Mail can be sent via local smtp or from an institutional smtp server. Configuration options are provided for authenticated sends and encryption of the outbound connection.

The amount and kind of mail coming from OAE can't currently be throttled. Keep an ear to your community's tolerance for automated messages from OAE. If you need to disable mail, one option is to configure your smtp server to capture messages from the OAE application server and redirect them to */dev/null*. An alternative is to leave the LiteOutgoingEmailMessageListener configuration in an ineffectual state. If you do, also set the maximum number of retries low and the interval between retries high in order to reduce the load of a subsystem you don't intend to make work.

Logging

Sakai OAE has multiple types of logs that it maintains. These should be monitored, and put on automatic rotation so as not to degrade system performance as they grow. It's so embarassing to lose a server because you let a log fill a disk.

The main Sakai OAE log is the by now familiar *nakamura/sling/logs/error.log*.

The solr indexing system, when run as an embedded part of the OAE jar, logs to *nakamura/sling/logs/solr.log*.

To see all logs generated by the core OSGi elements of OAE, check out the logging console in the Sling Web Console . Connect directly to *http://localhost:8080/system/console/slinglog* for the *error.log* and *solr.log* configurations and rotation status (see Figure 7-1). Click the wrench icon next to any entry to modify the production handling of logs. In particular, consider dropping the level of logging in the *error.log* from `Infor mation` to `Warnings`, or even all the way down to `Error`. (See Figure 7-2.)

The derby database logs in multiple locations: *nakamura/derby.log* and in the directories:

nakamura/sling/jackrabbit/version/db/log

nakamura/sling/jackrabbit/workspaces/default/db/log

nakamura/sling/jackrabbit/workspaces/security/db/log

nakamura/sling/sparsemap/db/log

That sums up all the OAE logs in the default out-of-the-box configuration. If you set up the *startup.sh* and *shutdown.sh* scripts in "Unix-Style Start and Stop Scripts" on page 99, then you'll also have a *run.log* in the *nakamura* directory.

As you add integrated systems such as a web server and database, or separate the user content, solr, and preview processor services, keep track of the growing collection of logs in your environment.

Reducing the JavaScript Debug Logging

By default, OAE is set to a relatively high level of JavaScript debugging output. To reduce this in production, modify the *sakai-ux/dev/configuration/config.js* file, setting `displayDebugInfo` to false. Setting this to false also removes the debugging `i18n_debug` language choice from the `Language` drop down list in the `My account Preferences` settings.

Create a Sakai User

Do it. If you didn't do it before, do it now. Sakai OAE should not be run as root or as the Windows admin user. The OAE service should not fail because they shut down your accounts if you change jobs.

Figure 7-1. The Sling Log console provides a quick overview of OAE OSGi logging

The Sakai user just has to be a regular operating account. Nothing specific to the Sakai OAE application will run on a privileged port (see Apache set up later at "Set Up a Web Server" on page 112 where OAE will be hitting a privileged port).

Unix-Style Start and Stop Scripts

Here is a very simple start script for use with */etc/init.d*. It expects to be called from the *nakamura* directory. Put the script in the *tools* directory with the name *startup.sh*. Make the file executable. Call it at the command line with `./tools/startup.sh`. The output is logged to a file called *run.log* in the *nakamura* directory. The file *OAE.pid* contains the process ID of nakamura, for use shutting it down:

```
#! /bin/sh

PROCESS_COUNT= \
```

```
`ps -ef | grep org.sakaiproject.nakamura.app-1.2.0.jar | grep -v grep | wc -l`
if [ $PROCESS_COUNT > 0 ]
then
  echo "Cowardly refusing to start nakamura in the belief"
  echo -n "an instance is already running"
  exit
fi

java -Dfile.encoding=UTF8 -Xmx512m -XX:MaxPermSize=256m -server -jar \
 app/target/org.sakaiproject.nakamura.app-1.2.0.jar 1>> run.log 2>&1 &
SAKAI_PID=$!
if [ -f OAE.pid ]
then
    rm OAE.pid
fi
echo $SAKAI_PID > OAE.pid
```

Figure 7-2. Reducing the logging level to Error greatly reduces the log size (and noise)

The equally simple shutdown script attempts to read the process ID from *OAE.pid* and to kill the associated process. Put this script in a file named *shutdown.sh* in the *tools* directory. Call it at the command line from the *nakamura* directory with `./tools/shut down.sh`:

```
#! /bin/sh
if [ -f OAE.pid ]
then
  SAKAI_PID=`cat OAE.pid`
  kill -9 $SAKAI_PID
```

```
   rm OAE.pid
else
   echo "No pid file found. Run 'ps -ef | grep "
   echo -n "nakamura' to identify the process to kill."
fi
```

The *shutdown.sh* script cleans up the *OAE.pid* file once it's no longer useful.

On Windows, use the service control manager of your choice to launch OAE using the *tools/run_debug.bat* job and to shutdown the associated task before system shutdown.

Integrating with a Database Backend

Not that derby's not a database. Derby is totally a database. Not many schools have highly trained Derby administrators though, and the Sakai OAE community has not sorted through performance issues related to Derby. The Derby database is a terrific solution for small scale demonstration pilots, but for production, you'll need another database.

Setting up OAE on a new backend is a highly destructive activity. All the data for your system is in the backing data store. Removing one and inserting another means starting from scratch. So, scratch it. It is technically sufficient to just remove the *sling* directory within the *nakamura* directory and restart OAE with a new database connector. However, if you've been working on customizations for a while, like play-doh pressed into the newspaper just one too many times, you may have some unexpected material left behind.

Choosing Your Database

The database choice you make for production will be influenced by license ownership, internal expertise, and institutional risk tolerance. If you have database administrators on staff whom you trust, then treat their recommendation with the most weight. They'll be the folks on whom you rely when a problem arises.

As of OAE version 1.2, the two databases of choice are PostgreSQL and Oracle. There exists a theoretical performance limitation in the way the datastore interacts with MySQL, though testing to prove (and mitigate) the bottleneck has not yet been performed. Active work is being done to test MongoDB as a backend store, and a handful of new contenders, such as Infinispan and Voldemort, are sneaking up.

Once you have chosen your database system, you'll need to choose a couple of settings:

Character set
> This should be unicode. UTF8 is a safe bet, but check with your database admininstrator on their best practice for international character set support.

Database user and password

> These credentials will be provided to OAE to create the database tables on install and then to maintain the data. The OAE user must have sufficient privileges to create tables at the time of install. If needed these permissions can be scaled back once the installation is complete.
>
> Under Oracle, the database user needs privileges to create tables, indices and sequences.
>
> Under PostgresSQL, the database user must be named "nakamura" and there must be a role by the name of "nakrole."

If there's something wonky going on in your database deployment, consult the underlying DDL and SQL for insights. Both the DDL and SQL syntax for each RDBMS are located in the sparsemapcontent code in the directory:

```
sparsemapcontent/drivers/jdbc/src/main/resources/org/sakaiproject/
nakamura/lite/storage/jdbc/config/
```

Much of your performance will rely on the tuning of the underlying database, and here a qualified database administrator can not be beat. As data accumulates from universities running OAE, recommendations for default tuning processes and settings will be documented. Consider sharing your experiences back to the community.

Integrating with PostgreSQL

PostgreSQL (often just called Postgres) is a free and open source relational database management system. It's pretty darn hardy. To exercise the integration with an offboard database, grab a copy of Postgres 9.1. The Postgres folks provide a terrific list of installation guides at *http://wiki.postgresql.org/wiki/Detailed_installation_guides*, and Enterprise DB maintains a collection of Postgres installers for most major operating systems at *http://www.enterprisedb.com/products-services-training/pgdownload*.

Be sure to check the README file with the installer. For example on Mac OS X, you'll need to modify the default system memory settings before installing Postgres.

Initialize a small and terribly insecure database instance with the *initdb* command in your Postgres *bin* directory. Provide a directory location for data storage. In order to support a variety of languages, set the default locale and encoding to appropriate unicode values:

```
postgresdir/bin/initdb --locale=en_US.UTF-8
        --encoding=UNICODE
        --pgdata=/Users/username/postgres/dbdata
```

This creates a Postgres database in the directory */Users/username/postgres/dbdata*, which will run on port 5432.

If the installer started up a database, shut it down before creating your Sakai OAE focused one:

```
sudo su - postgres
postgresdir/bin/pg_ctl stop -D/Library/PostgreSQL/9.1/data/

waiting for server to shut down.... done
server stopped
```

Swap back to your normal Sakai user, and start up this new clean database server:

```
        postgresdir/bin/pg_ctl -D \
/Users/username/postgres/dbdata -l \
/Users/username/postgres/db_logfile start
```

If you're still the Postgres user when you attempt to create a mini database in your Sakai user's directory space, you might receive an error of the kind *pg_ctl: could not open PID file "/Users/username/postgres/dbdata/postmaster.pid": Permission denied.* Just be sure you are the Sakai user, and the permissions will be fine.

Create a database within the service:

postgresdir/bin/createdb sakaioae

Login with the Postgres interactive SQL interpeter to create the users who will talk to OAE. Note that you are not prompted to login. This is a really small and really insecure database for demonstration purposes.

postgresdir/bin/psql --dbname=sakaioae

```
psql (9.1.3)
Type "help" for help.

postgres=#
```

Create two users, one named nakamura and the other nakrole. The DDL scripts for OAE are expecting these actual names. Give these users adequate privileges to set up the database and subsequently read and write to it.

postgres=# CREATE USER nakamura WITH PASSWORD 'password';

postgres=# CREATE USER nakrole WITH PASSWORD 'password';

postgres=# GRANT ALL PRIVILEGES ON DATABASE sakaioae TO nakamura;

postgres=# GRANT ALL PRIVILEGES ON DATABASE sakaioae TO nakrole;

On successful creation, postgres returns the message CREATE ROLE for user creation and simply GRANT for privilege granting.

To quit, use the \q command:

postgres=# \q

Before hooking OAE up, make sure the database created properly:

***postgresdir*/bin/psql --dbname=sakaioae --username=nakamura**

Once connected, use the \list psql command to see all the databases your nakamura user has access to. The *sakaioae* database will appear in this list.

postgres=# \list

```
                        List of databases
    Name   | Owner | Encoding |  Collate   |   Ctype    | Access privileges
-----------+-------+----------+------------+------------+-------------------
 postgres  | user  | UTF8     | en_US.UTF-8 | en_US.UTF-8 |
 sakaioae  | user  | UTF8     | en_US.UTF-8 | en_US.UTF-8 | =Tc/user         +
           |       |          |            |            | user=CTc/user    +
           |       |          |            |            | sakai=CTc/user
```

then use the Postgres-specific command to list all tables in the *sakaioae* database:

sakaioae=> \dt;

```
    No relations found.
```

You can also can use a select statement to check the same thing.

select schemaname,tablename from pg_tables where schemaname='nakamura';

which at present should similarly show you an empty system:

```
    schemaname | tablename
    -----------+-----------
    (0 rows)
```

Make sure your OAE is completely shut down. There's nothing so ugly as ripping the innards out of a running system. Subdirectories will start appearing ghostlike as the running code in memory tries to recover from the loss of its body. Once OAE is shutdown, remove the nakamura directory and rebuild from the source code ZIP file.

 Here is a cheat sheet for rebuilding nakamura clean:

```
cd source
rm -R nakamura
unzip sakaiproject-nakamura-nakamura-1.2.0-0-g33d7e98.zip
mv sakaiproject-nakamura-6407909 nakamura
cd nakamura
export MAVEN_OPTS="-Xmx256m -XX:PermSize=256m"
mvn clean install
```

This should take about a half-hour to complete, as all the required Maven artifacts have already been retrieved on the initial build back in "Building from Source" on page 15.

The final step before starting OAE up is to configure the JDBC connection parameters for your little demo Postgres database. Like disabling the self-registration service in section "Removing the Self-Service Functions" on page 85, this configuration is done in the *load* directory, within the *nakamura* directory. The configuration file to create exactly matches the name of the JDBC bundle.

cd nakamura

mkdir load; cd load

vi org.sakaiproject.nakamura.lite.storage.jdbc.JDBCStorageClientPool.cfg

Insert the contents:

```
jdbc-driver=org.postgresql.Driver
jdbc-url=jdbc:postgresql://localhost:5432/sakaioae?autoReconnectForPools\=true
username=nakamura
password=password
```

This *.cfg* file must be precise. The Felix file reader is pretty finicky. There can be no trailing spaces or invisible characters. If you get an error like *java.lang.ClassNotFoundException: org.postgresql.Driver not found by postgresqljdbc* check for a trailing space on the entries in the *.cfg* file.

Tail the database log db_logfile while you start Sakai OAE up.

tail -f /Users/*username*/postgres/db_logfile

You'll eventually see an entry in the database log like the following:

```
ERROR:  relation "css" does not exist at character 22
STATEMENT:  select count(*) from css
```

The select statement on the CSS table is a check for the existence of the database tables. When OAE receives the error that no such table exists, it creates the data schema in Postgres. Start up may well be preternaturally slow, as you are now running both a database and your OAE locally. Sit back and wait. If your LDAP server is running from "Set Up a Mini LDAP Instance" on page 65, you might want to shut that down. Your database is small. The startup cost is high.

The sling/logs/error.log will tell you when it's done:

```
*INFO* [FelixDispatchQueue] org.apache.felix.framework FrameworkEvent STARTLEVEL
CHANGED
```

Be patient. Wait for the system to finish loading. There's an unpleasant truth to admit at this point. Correct load up takes a long time. If you access the system prematurely, it may fail to fully load. This is terrifying, inappropriate, and just plain bad form. Nonetheless, it's true. The good news is that once the system is started there are very few reasons to shut it down. Much of the system configuration is done live in the OSGi system console.

If you're twitchy and need to do something (other than a crossword puzzle) while it fully starts, you can watch the system console Components screen at *http://localhost: 8080/system/console/components*. OAE is up and running when the list of components with a status of *unsatisfied* drops to just 3: the `RequestLoggerService`, `FsResourcePro vider`, and `TrustedLoginTokenProxyPostProcessor`.

At this point take a look at two items:

1. In the database, query for a count of items in one of the content storage tables:

   ***postgresdir*/bin/psql --dbname=sakaioae --username=nakamura**

   sakaioae=> select count(*) from ac_css_b;

   ```
   count
   -------
       5
   ```

   Now, create a user, login in to the frontend of OAE, and upload a file. Run the query again, and you'll see the value has increased (though not necessarily by a single digit).

   ```
   count
   -------
       9
   ```

2. On disk, in your *nakamura* directory, notice there is a new directory called *store*. When you upload a file, the informational data about it is stored in the database, but the file itself is stored on disk. OAE-created documents are stored directly in the database, unless they get quite large, then they are treated like uploaded files. The definition of very large and the location to store the material are both configurable. By default, very large is 16 Kb, and the storage location is *store* within *nakamura*. When scaling up, consider mounting the */store* directory on network attached storage, so it can easily grow independent of your application server.

To change Postgres parameters once installed, you can use the OSGi web console, just as you did with the Sakai User Servlet configuration once it was initialized in "Removing the Self-Service Functions" on page 85. Connect to the Configuration tab of the OSGi dashboard at *http://localhost:8080/system/console/ConfigMgr* and click on the pencil button for `org.sakaiproject.nakamura.lite.storage.jdbc.JDBCStorageClientPool` `.cfg`. See Figure 7-3.

Modifying the JDBC configuration here has the effect of updating two files on disk: one the original configuration file you created in the *load* directory, and the other a *.config* suffixed equivalent in the *sling/config* directory structure.

By creating the configuration file on disk while OAE is not running, OAE reads in the database configuration information as it starts up, creating database tables as part of the initialization process. Without the configuration file the default configuration would kick in, creating tables in an Apache Derby database. If you then configure Postgres interactively, OAE creates a fresh set of tables in that database. The Postgres system becomes the datastore OAE relies on, but there's a vestigal Derby database lying around.

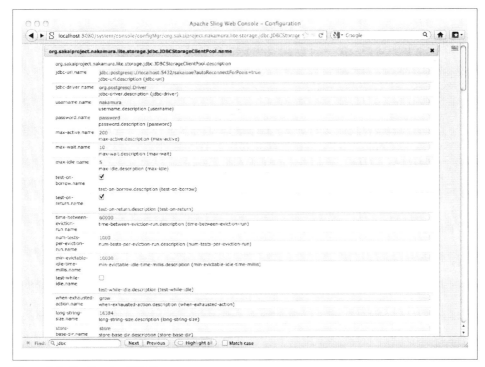

Figure 7-3. Configuring JDBC

Integrating with Oracle

Oracle has a proprietary JDBC connector, freely available to Oracle clients. In order to install Oracle as a backend, the appropriate JDBC jar must be obtained from Oracle, and then built locally. This makes it a bit more complicated than working with an open source database, for which drivers can be precompiled and packaged up in the OAE distribution.

Obtain an Oracle instance and empowered user

Sakai OAE is being used in production at schools running Oracle versions 10g and 11g. The configuration is slightly different for the 10 and 11 series. Before you get started, get in touch with your database team and request an Oracle instance with an associated user, empowered to create tables and indices, and to read and write data. You'll need to know the following information:

Oracle version to the fourth or fifth place
11.2.0.3 is meaningfully different from 11.7.0.1. For the 11g series you'll need to provide the version number to the Maven pom when you build the Oracle driver bundle. For the 10g series, the exact version number is less important.

Hostname, port and Oracle instance identifier (SID) or service name
> The hostname, port, and Oracle SID or service name form the JDBC URL by which OAE connects to Oracle. The default port is 1521.

User name and password
> Though some DBAs will refer to the Oracle user as the Oracle schema, the two are not quite synonymous. It will suffice under either title, providing there exists a user who can connect, create and drop tables and indices, and can read and write data.

The next item to obtain is the appropriate Oracle JDBC driver and to wrap it for OAE. You may already have the driver as part of your licensed Oracle database. If you don't have that handy, connect to Oracle's website (*http://www.oracle.com/technetwork/database/features/jdbc/index-091264.html*), and download the JDBC driver appropriate for your version of Oracle. A rule of thumb is to use *ojdbc14.jar* for the Oracle 10 series and *ojdbc6.jar* for the Oracle 11 series.

Oracle 10: Build sparsemapcontent and nakamura with the ojdbc14.jar

Grab the sparse code from *https://github.com/sakaiproject/sparsemapcontent/tree/org.sakaiproject.nakamura.core-1.3.4*. Click the ZIP button to download a zipball of sparsemapcontent. Unzip the sparsemapcontent source code into your *source* directory, at a level parallel to where you've been working with *nakamura*. Move it to a human readable name, like *sparsemap*. Copy the *ojdbc14.jar* driver to the sparsemap directory, and install it into your Maven repository:

```
mvn install:install-file -Dfile=ojdbc14.jar -DgroupId=com.oracle \
-DartifactId=ojdbc -Dversion=1.4 -Dpackaging=jar
```

This Maven command installs a new artifact in the repository with an associated pom file of `ojdbc/1.4/ojdbc-1.4.pom`, showing the artifact name and version number. This gets picked up in the bundle build.

Modify the *pom.xml* in the *sparsemap* directory. Uncomment the entry for the ojdbc artifact, so `ojdbc` gets built and loaded by Maven when it builds:

```
<dependency>
  <groupId>com.oracle</groupId>
  <artifactId>ojdbc</artifactId>
  <version>1.4</version>
</dependency>
```

Now make a clean install in the sparsemap directory.

```
cd sparsemap
```

```
mvn clean install
```

This will build in about two minutes, and stow the artifact in your Maven repository. Once your OJDBC jar for sparsemapcontent is built, the next step is to build it in nakamura.

Now that the sparsemap bundle is built with Oracle, rebuild nakamura both to rely on the Oracle driver and to include the new sparsemap driver. First, build the nakamura version of the OJDBC bundle. Like the sparsemap bundle, this gets built in a specific directory, configured by a small pom dedicated to bundling just this driver. The location is the *contrib/oracle-jdbc* directory within *nakamura*. Copy the same *ojdbc14.jar* into the *nakamura/contrib/oracle-jdbc* directory that you downloaded and put in the *sparsemap* directory. Change to the *oracle-jdbc* directory and build the bundle:

```
cd nakamura/contrib/oracle-jdbc
```

```
mvn clean install
```

In order to include this new JDBC bundle in OAE, edit the *list.xml* file to indicate the OJDBC driver instead of the Postgres wrapper. The *list.xml* file is in *nakamura* in the *app/src/main/bundles* directory. Edit the *list.xml* file to replace postgreswrapper with the correct JDBC. In the following section:

```
<bundle>
  <groupId>org.sakaiproject.nakamura</groupId>
  <artifactId>org.sakaiproject.nakamura.postgresqlwrapper</artifactId>
  <version>1.2.0</version>
</bundle>
```

change the *artifactId* value to org.sakaiproject.nakamura.ojdbc:

```
<bundle>
  <groupId>org.sakaiproject.nakamura</groupId>
  <artifactId>org.sakaiproject.nakamura.ojdbc</artifactId>
  <version>1.2.0</version>
</bundle>
```

Notice that in this instance the version number is 1.2.0, which corresponds to the nakamura versioning, not 1.4, which corresponds to the versioning within sparsemap-content. Now that the correct JDBC is indicated, rebundle nakamura:

```
cd nakamura
```

```
mvn -Pbundle clean install
```

It should clock in at about four minutes.

Oracle 11: Build nakamura with the ojdbc6.jar

For Oracle 11 versions the sparsemapcontent bundle does not need to be independently built, as it does with Oracle 10. However, a revised *pom.xml* file for the *oracle-jdbc-6* bundle is required. You can download the *pom.xml* from the O'Reilly website for this book at *http://shop.oreilly.com/product/0636920023241.do*. It's about 200 lines, covering Oracle versions 11.1.0.6, 11.1.0.7, 11.2.0.1.0, 11.2.0.2.0, and 11.2.0.3.

The OJDBC6 bundle for use with Oracle 11 gets built in the *contrib/oracle-jdbc-6* directory within *nakamura*. Copy the revised *pom.xml* and your *ojdbc6.jar* driver into this directory, overwriting the *pom.xml* already present there. Change into the *oracle-jdbc-6* directory and install the *ojdbc6.jar* driver in the Maven repository:

```
cd nakamura/contrib/oracle-jdbc-6
```

```
        mvn install:install-file -Dfile=ojdbc6.jar \
    -DgroupId=com.oracle -DartifactId=ojdbc6 -Dversion=oracle11version \
    -Dpackaging=jar -P oracle11version
```

Replace *oracle11version* in the `version` and `P` parameters with the actual version number for your Oracle instance, for example `11.2.0.2.0`. The P parameter designates which of the five profiles in the *pom.xml* to act on. This Maven command installs a new artifact with an associated pom in the repository reflecting the artifact name and version number, for example ojdbc6/11.2.0.2.0/ojdbc-11.2.0.2.0.pom.

Now build the OJDBC6 bundle for nakamura. Again, replace *oracle11version* in the example with your actual Oracle version number.

```
mvn -P oracle11version clean install
```

This will build in about a minute and stow the OJDBC6 artifact in your Maven repository.

In order to include this new bundle in OAE, edit the *list.xml* file to indicate the ojdbc6 driver instead of the postgres wrapper. The *list.xml* file is in *nakamura* in the *app/src/main/bundles* directory. Edit the *list.xml* file to replace `postgreswrapper` with ojdbc6. In the following section:

```
<bundle>
  <groupId>org.sakaiproject.nakamura</groupId>
  <artifactId>org.sakaiproject.nakamura.postgresqlwrapper</artifactId>
  <version>1.2.0</version>
</bundle>
```

replace the artifactId with ojdbc6. Notice that in this instance the version number is 1.2.0, which corresponds to the nakamura version number, not the Oracle 11 version number.

```
<bundle>
  <groupId>org.sakaiproject.nakamura</groupId>
  <artifactId>org.sakaiproject.nakamura.ojdbc6</artifactId>
  <version>1.2.0</version>
</bundle>
```

Now that the correct JDBC is indicated, rebundle nakamura:

```
cd nakamura
```

```
mvn -Pbundle clean install
```

It will take just a few minutes to build.

Configure the Oracle connection

The connection configuration is that same for both Oracle 10 and 11. Create a directory in the *nakamura* directory where OAE will find the Oracle configuration parameters. The filename matches the JDBC connector, and the directory structure reflects the full package name:

cd nakamura/

mkdir -p sling/config/org/sakaiproject/nakamura/lite/storage/jdbc

With the editor of your choice create the file

sling/config/org/sakaiproject/nakamura/lite/storage/jdbc/JDBCStorageClientPool

.config

Put the contents for your database connection in this file. The values for `jdbc-driver` and `service.pid` should be exactly as shown. The `jdbc-url`, `username`, and `password` will be specific to your Oracle installation. If your Oracle instance uses a service name instead of an Oracle SID to connect, then the syntax will be slightly different on the JDBC URL parameter: `jdbc:oracle:thin:@//`*machine.example.edu*`:1521/`*SERVICE_NAME*.

```
jdbc-driver="oracle.jdbc.driver.OracleDriver"
service.pid="org.sakaiproject.nakamura.lite.storage.jdbc.JDBCStorageClientPool"
jdbc-url="jdbc:oracle:thin:@machine.example.edu:1521:SID"
password="pass"
username="user"
```

Save this file, and the system is ready to start up and populate the Oracle schema.

Where, Oh, Where Has My CFG Gone? Oh, Where, Oh Where Could It Be?

Sakai OAE accepts configuration on components in three ways: through *.config* files in deep directories within the *sling/config* directory, through *.cfg* files in the *load* directory and interactively via the Sling web console.

.config files in sling/config
> The OSGi Configuration Admin service reads in configuration information from the *sling/config* directory structures when Sakai OAE first starts up. Configuration is on a per bundle basis, with the filename matching the class name and the directory structure matching the package name. For example, for the Oracle sample the *JDBCStorageClientPool.config* file is stored in *sling/config/org/sakaiproject/nakamura/lite/storage/jdbc*. These configuration files support robust property setting options, including identifying the dataype of a value, and permitting non-scalar values for properties. The full specification for what is permitted in a *.config* file is provided by the Felix *ConfigurationHandler* class.

Start OAE up

Start Sakai OAE from the *nakamura* directory. The system will detect there is no schema in Oracle, and will build one fresh. In the primary log at *nakamura/sling/logs/error.log*, you'll eventually see an entry like the following:

```
*INFO* [FelixStartLevel]
org.sakaiproject.nakamura.lite.storage.jdbc.JDBCStorageClient Schema does not exist
ORA-00942: table or view does not exist
```

This is the signal to OAE that it has connected to a fresh new database and should build its infrastructure. The next series of log entries show each table as it is created.

If you get an error of the form `Unresolved constraint in bundle org.sakaiproject.naka mura.ojdbc6` on a package such as `oracle.aurora.rdbms` or `xdb.jar`, there is probably a problem with the file as installed to the Maven repository. Having to manually install to the repository is one of the challenges of working with a proprietary driver set. Cleaning out your Maven repository in *.m2/repository* will usually clear this error up, though it does mean a time consuming rebuild of the repository the next time you build.

Set Up a Web Server

Use the Apache http server version 2 for the frontend service. There's no reason to gesture to other web servers. It is well resolved that there's one true (open source) web server, and it is Apache.

These examples use Apache HTTP Server version 2.2, but here, again, defer to your trusted system administrator. They'll be up to date on all the trade-offs on versions and builds. In production, Apache should be configured to run SSL'd on port 443. This section just covers the conversation between Apache and OAE, leaving the remaining points of Apache configuration up to your local established practice.

Apache accepts connections on port 80, which is the default http port. Up until now you've been accessing OAE on *localhost* with the port number 8080. Only privileged users are allowed to access the well known ports below 1024. The Apache http web server will take requests on port 80 (or 443 once it is SSL'd) and forward them to OAE on port 8080.

Retrieve Apache and Install Modules

On Linux flavors use apt-get, or the package manager of your choice, to install Apache:

```
sudo apt-get install apache2
```

Mac OS X conveniently comes with a preinstalled instance of Apache 2.2.1. To turn it on, go to the `System Preferences` panel and click `Sharing`. Check the box for `Web Shar ing`. Once enabled, the System Preferences panel will show you the URLs by which you can access your local Apache http server. The loopback interfaces of *http://127.0.0.1* and *http://localhost* will pretty much always work.

There are five apache modules generally used with OAE to both speed up delivery and set appropriate redirects: `cache`, `proxy_http`, `expires`, `mem_cache`, and `rewrite`. To see which modules are loaded use the `-M` flag:

```
httpd -M
```

On flavors of Unix you can enable these with:

```
/usr/sbin/a2enmod cache
/usr/sbin/a2enmod proxy_http
/usr/sbin/a2enmod expires
/usr/sbin/a2enmod mem_cache
/usr/sbin/a2enmod rewrite
```

To find your *httpd.conf* file, as well as other details on your install use the `-V` flag:

```
httpd -V
```

This will tell you where to find your *httpd.conf* file:

```
-D SERVER_CONFIG_FILE="/private/etc/apache2/httpd.conf"
```

Make a note also of where your logs are located:

```
-D DEFAULT_ERRORLOG="logs/error_log"
```

Virtual Host Configuration

In the *httpd.conf* file, or the *hostnamed* file in the *sites-available* directory, add an entry for your primary application server node, designating the name, document root, and log locations. Set up some reasonably restrictive Location rules, and configure the proxy module to redirect all traffic on 80 over to 8080:

```
<VirtualHost *:80>
      ServerAdmin webmaster@example.edu
      ServerName example.edu
      ServerAlias www.example.edu
      DocumentRoot /srv/www/example.edu/public_html/
      ErrorLog /srv/www/example.edu.com/logs/error.log
      CustomLog /srv/www/example.edu/logs/access.log combined
      ProxyRequests Off
      <Location />
            Order deny,allow
            Allow from all
            Options none
      </Location>
      ProxyPass / http://127.0.0.1:8080/
      ProxyPassReverse / http://127.0.0.1:8080/
      ProxyPreserveHost On
</VirtualHost>
```

The document root in the virtual host configuration will be ignored most of the time, as everything ends up coming from OAE. If you bring OAE down for maintenance this is a handy place to put an elevator music *index.html*. Comment out the ProxyPass elements of the VirtualHost configuration, making the document root meaningful again. Here's a favorite holding pattern page:

```
<center>This system is temporarily b0rked.<br><br>
<img src="http://farm4.staticflickr.com/3182/2988617774_8b3ed0d0b0_d.jpg"
alt="Image Created by Max Feiger original at http://www.flickr.com/photos/
sleeper-cell/2988617774/ used under Creative Commons Attribtion Share Alike
license"> </center>
```

Server Protection Service Configuration

There's another piece to the Apache configuration: the Server Protection Service. This service limits exposure to cross-site scripting attacks by preventing content uploaded by the folks using your system from accessing the core functionality of the system. All access to uploaded content goes through a secondary network interface.

The preferred method of configuring the Server Protection Service is to set up a subdomain or an entirely separate virtual host for serving content uploaded by the people using OAE. If the primary OAE application server is named example.edu, then a common model is to name the second application server content.example.edu.

Connect to the Sling OSGi web console at *http://localhost:8080/system/console*, and click the Configuration tab. Scroll down to the Sakai Nakamura :: Server Protection

Service component and click on the pencil icon to open up the configuration screen. Leave the Trusted Content Paths at their default values. For Trusted Hosts, click the "+" button to add a trusted host. Enter a line redirecting from the OAE domain name to the content subdomain:

example.edu = http://content.example.edu:8082

Be sure to retain the default setting for localhost:8080 = http://localhost:8082 as well. See Figure 7-4.

You must set a Trusted Secret value. This value is used to encrypt tokens that transfer identity from the trusted host to the user content host. The trusted secret value is the same on both application servers.

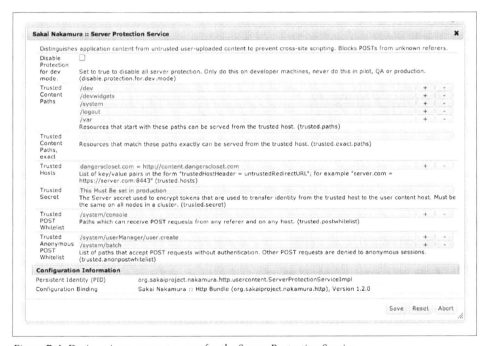

Figure 7-4. Designating a content server for the Server Protection Service

The virtual host configuration for the content serving host is almost, but not quite, identical to the main application node. In particular, all incoming traffic on port 80 is sent to port 8082 on the content host, instead of to 8080:

```
<VirtualHost *:80>
    ServerAdmin webmaster@content.example.edu
    ServerName content.example.edu
    DocumentRoot /srv/www/content.example.edu/public_html/
    ErrorLog /srv/www/content.example.edu/logs/error.log
    CustomLog /srv/www/content.example.edu/logs/access.log combined
    ProxyRequests Off
```

```
<Location />
    Order deny,allow
    Allow from all
    Options none
</Location>
ProxyPass / http://127.0.0.1:8082/
ProxyPassReverse / http://127.0.0.1:8082/
ProxyPreserveHost On
</VirtualHost>
```

Setting up a separate content node has the additional advantage of providing two sets of logs: one with standard activity, one just logging content downloads—though those downloads are slightly unintelligible without cross referencing to the application logs.

The less preferred method of configuring the Server Protection Service is to simply redirect the port 8080 on your application node to port 8082 on the same node. In this case the trusted host entry would look like:

example.edu:8080 = http://example.edu:8082

The Preview Processor

The preview processor produces thumbnail and in-system displays of many file types. This vastly improves the user experience in OAE, allowing people to browse materials in context without having to download files. The preview processor installation is somewhat brittle still. To get it set up on OAE version 1.2 you'll need to set up an Ubuntu 10.10 or later server, or be ready to wrestle somewhat with Ruby to satisfy dependencies.

1. Install puppet:

   sudo apt-get install puppet

2. Use puppet to install dependencies.

   Create a script called **preview_processor.pp** on the Ubuntu 10.10 or later machine:

   ```
   # tested on ubuntu 10.10
   # run using the following command :
   # sudo puppet apply preview_processor.pp
   #

   $preview_processor_packages = [
     'graphicsmagick', 'libcurl4-openssl-dev', 'libmagickcore-dev',
     'libmagickwand-dev', 'ruby1.8-dev', 'rubygems1.8',
     'poppler-utils', 'pdftk', 'librmagick-ruby1.8', 'tesseract-ocr',
     'openoffice.org', 'openoffice.org-java-common'
   ]


   package { $preview_processor_packages:
     ensure   => installed,
   }
   ```

```
package { 'docsplit':
  ensure   => '0.5.2',
  provider => gem,
  require  => Package['rubygems1.8'],
}

package { 'json':
  ensure   => installed,
  provider => gem,
  require  => [ Package["rubygems1.8"], Package["ruby1.8-dev"] ],
}
```

3. As root, call this new puppet script:

puppet apply preview_processor.pp

If you need the `apply` parameter when you call the *preview_processor.pp* then you know you're on the right version of puppet.

4. As a less powerful user, start up Open Office in headless mode in the background:

soffice --headless
--accept="socket,host=127.0.0.1,port=8100;urp;" --nofirststartwizard &

5. Run the preview processor:

cd source/nakamura/scripts/

ruby preview_processor.rb -s http://example.edu:8080/ -p admin

6. In the web browser of your choice upload a PDF document. The preview processor logs the injest of the file, and the posting back of the completed thumbnails:

```
INFO -- : Starts a new batch of queued files: lYzoi8FMec
INFO -- : processing lYzoi8FMec
INFO -- : with filename: lYzoi8FMec.pdf
INFO -- : Generate tags for lYzoi8FMec, /tags/edu oracle/tags/network diagram/
tags/authentication systems/tags/command ldap/tags/java version
INFO -- : Uploaded image to curl http://example.edu:8080/p/lYzoi8FMec/
page1.large.jpg
INFO -- : Uploaded image to curl http://example.edu:8080/p/lYzoi8FMec/
page1.normal.jpg
INFO -- : Uploaded image to curl http://example.edu:8080/p/lYzoi8FMec/
page1.small.jpg
```

7. Reload OAE in your browser, and you'll see the beautiful previews.

Separating Solr

The Solr search library is embedded within Sakai OAE by default. It provides fast access to elements stored in the sparsemapcontent column oriented data store. Some universities have seen faster response times from their system by setting up a dedicated Solr server, separate from the OAE application.

To go this route fire up a separate application server, for example, `solr.example.edu`. Shut down any nakamura you might have running before you get started, so you're in a clean state.

Download the OAE specific build of prerelease Solr version 4 from http://source.sa-kaiproject.org/release/oae/solr/solr-example.tar.gz   (*http://source.sakaiproject.org/release/oae/solr/solr-example.tar.g*).

Create a *solr* directory on your `solr.example.edu` server, and unzip the tarball there, to generate a directory named *example* within the *solr* directory. This *example* directory structure is drawn directly from the Apache Solr suggested setup, and is going to be the actual Solr setup, not merely an example one:

```
mkdir -p source/solr
```

```
mv solr-example.tar.gz solr
```

```
cd solr
```

```
tar -xzvf solr-example.tar.gz
```

There, now you have a directory structure like:

```
source/
   solr/
      example/
```

Retrieve the configuration files from the OAE 1.2 release area at *https://github.com/sakaiproject/solr/tree/org.sakaiproject.nakamura.solr-1.4.2*. Click the `ZIP` button at that location to retrieve the configuration files. This will get you a ZIP file:

sakaiproject-solr-org.sakaiproject.nakamura.solr-1.4.2-0-g23dfa59.zip

Unzip this one in your *source* directory:

```
cd source
```

```
unzip sakaiproject-solr-org.sakaiproject.nakamura.solr-1.4.2-0-g23dfa59.zip
```

Make the configuration directory:

```
mkdir -p solr/conf
```

Copy just the configuration files from *resources* to the `solr/conf` directory:

```
cp -pr sakaiproject-solr-7404157/src/main/resources/* solr/conf
```

Now, you'll have a directory structure like:

```
source/
   solr/
      example/
      conf/
```

From the example directory, as a non-root user, start it up. Note that the `solr` `.solr.home` value is the directory where you just unzipped the configuration files:

```
cd solr/example
```

```
    java -Dsolr.solr.home=/Users/username/source/solr \
-Djetty.port=8983 -jar start.jar 1> run.log 2>&1 &
```

The solr service creates a data directory once it starts up. Now, you'll have a directory structure like:

```
source/
    solr/
        example/
        conf/
        data/
```

The *run.log* is in the *example* directory, from where the Java process was kicked off. Good output looks like this:

```
INFO: SolrDispatchFilter.init() done
INFO::Started SocketConnector@0.0.0.0:8983
org.apache.solr.core.SolrCore execute
INFO: [] webapp=null path=null params={start=0&event=firstSearcher&q=solr
+rocks&rows=10} hits=0 status=0 QTime=53
org.apache.solr.core.SolrCore execute
INFO: [] webapp=null path=null params=
{event=firstSearcher&q=static+firstSearcher+warming+query+from+solrconfig.xml}
hits=0 status=0 QTime=5
org.apache.solr.core.QuerySenderListener newSearcher
INFO: QuerySenderListener done.
org.apache.solr.core.SolrCore registerSearcher
INFO: [] Registered new searcher Searcher@f102d3 main
```

Check the solr setup via a web browser by accessing *http://solr.example.edu:8983/solr*. You should get a nice solr interface at that URL (see Figure 7-5).

Next is to configure the main OAE application server to reach out to the remote Solr indexer before starting OAE up.

1. Create a file named *org.sakaiproject.nakamura.solr.RemoteSolrClient.cfg* in the na-kamura *load* directory with the single line: `remoteurl = http://solr.example.edu:8983/solr`

2. Create a file named *org.sakaiproject.nakamura.solr.SolrServerServiceImpl.cfg* in the nakamura *load* directory with the single line: `solr-impl = remote`

3. Start up OAE.

Solr indexing will now occur on the `solr.example.edu` host, while the application work occurs on your main host.

The query time out on the standalone solr server may need to be configured from the default of 1 second. If you see an error message in the sling error log of the type:

```
No live SolrServers available to handle this request (500)
```

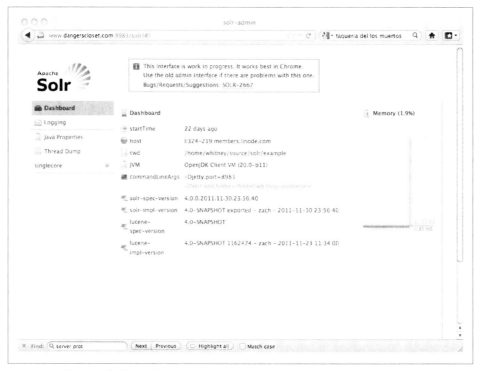

Figure 7-5. The Solr dashboard

then modify the `MultiMasterRemoteSolrClient` settings, increasing the `query-so-time out` value from 1 second to something larger. You can do this live in the OSGi web console once Sakai OAE is running. Connect to the console at *http://localhost:8080/ system/console/configMgr*. Scroll down to the `org.sakaiproject.nakamura.solr.Multi MasterRemoteSolrClient.name` component and click the pencil icon to open up the configuration screen. Modify the value for `query-so-timeout.name` from `1000` to `10000`.

Starting Clean

Sometimes, as you're working, you'll make an error so unpleasant and unforeseen that you don't know where to start finding it. Before you back all the way out and rebuild the front and backends from scratch, here are some interim steps:

Start over with clean frontend code
If you were working in JavaScript when something went haywire, your best first step is to wipe out the folders *sakai-ux/dev* and *sakai-ux/devwidgets* and unzip the frontend code fresh. This will impact changes you've made to your CSS, *config.js*, *custom_config.js*, label customization in *bundle/default.properties* as well as any widgets you've downloaded and installed. Back up your customizations and reintroduce them one at a time until you reproduce the problem.

Clean out the sling directory

> If you have not yet configured an external database, then it's often sufficient to remove the *sling* directory within the *nakamura* directory. On startup OAE rebuilds the Derby database and supporting content from scratch. Removing the *sling* directory will remove customizations made via the OSGi web console, including File System Resource entries directing the frontend to customized *dev* and *dev-widgets*, any LDAP and database integration, and things like email settings and even the admin password, which goes back to the default on a clean rebuild. Configuration files with the *.cfg* format in the *load* directory are untouched, because they are parallel to the sling directory. Any *.config* file in the *sling/config* directory structure will need to be recreated manually before startup.
>
> This is the nuclear option.

Drop your database and rebuild both frontend and backend from scratch

> In the worst of cases, you've integrated to an external database, and something has gone seriously mushroom shaped with subsequent customization work. You can try cleaning just the frontend code in *sakai-ux* and restarting. If that doesn't work, just removing the sling directory won't be sufficient—the database is hanging onto state information. You can try dropping and recreating the database and removing the *sling* directory, but at that level of complexity it's just as easy to rebuild from scratch. Grab a copy of any configuration files you've put in your *nakamura/load* directory to speed up the reconfiguration. Drop the database, recreate your database user(s), and rebuild.
>
> This is the global thermonuclear war option.

The Checklist

There's a lot that's been going on in this chapter. Atul Gawande's *The Checklist Manifesto* makes a great case for how simple lists can effectively manage complexity. Here's a checklist for production deployment:

1. Create an OS user to run everything for you.
2. Get all your ports opened. (See Table 7-1.)
3. Choose and configure your database.
4. Install OAE. If the loopback interface is inaccessible for some reason, configure the Server Protection Service while you work issues out with the database setup.
5. Change the admin password.
6. Setup Apache, your content host configuration, and modify ServerProtectionService to your production format.
7. Set up a separate solr indexer, if desired.
8. Set up the preview processor.
9. Configure email.

10. Apply all your UI customizations, sorted out in Chapter 4.

11. Set up LDAP authentication, sorted out in Chapter 5.

12. Modify the JavaScript debug level, removing *i18n debug* from the list of languages.

13. Set up log monitoring and rotation on the OAE and Apache logs on the primary application server, the OAE and Apache logs on the content server, the database logs, preview processor logs, and the solr logs. Reduce the logging level for OSGi.

14. Set up start and stop scripts for when your machines restart.

15. Take a snapshot of all the configuration files, so you can easily redeploy, should you need to.

16. Draw yourself a local node and network diagram. It'll help you remember what and where everything is six months from now when you want to expand or upgrade. See Figure 7-6.

A production environment for OAE can be as highly complex as a set of clustered nodes for every separatable service in the system or as simple as the binary install in "Binary Install" on page 8.

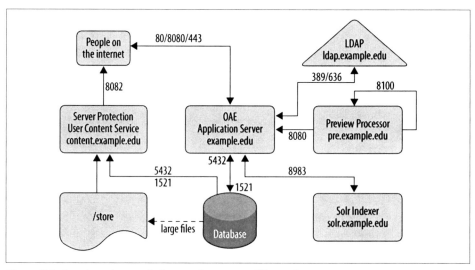

Figure 7-6. A node and network diagram for one possible production environment

Table 7-1. The Ports

Port	Purpose
port 80	Standard http port, configured in Apache virtual host entry to forward to 8080
port 443	Standard https port, configured in Apache virtual host entry to forward to 80/8080
port 8080	Sakai OAE application port; if the preview processor is on a separate machine, it needs to communicate with the OAE application server on 8080

Port	Purpose
port 8082	Sakai OAE content port; user uploaded files are delivered on port 8082, rather than on the application code port of 8080
port 25 or 587	Outbound email port; port 25 is the standard for SMTP; port 587 is often enabled instead for email submission in order to reduce spam distribution on the standard SMTP port
port 389 or 636	LDAP port for contacting the authentication service; port 636 is the standard encrypted LDAPS port; clear transmission on port 389 should be avoided
port 1521	Default Oracle JDBC port
port 5432	Default PostgreSQL JDBC port
port 8983	Solr communication port, if you set up a separate solr server
port 8100	Expected port for the preview processor to communicate with Open Office on the same host; this port need not be opened to extra-host communication

About the Author

Max Whitney is the Technical Team Lead for enterprise academic services in ITS at New York University and an active member in the DIY technology communities in New York. She managed the Blackboard implementation at NYU from 2001 to 2009, acting as the technical lead for an enterprise upgrade impacting 110,000 users in 2008. She led a Sakai CLE pilot (then known as Sakai v2) at NYU in 2007, and is the technical architect on NYU's launch of Sakai OAE in 2011. She served on the Sakai Product Council 2010-2011 and is a member of the Sakai OAE Technical Review Board. She received her M.S. in Computer Science at NYU's Courant Institute of Mathematical Sciences and B.A. from Columbia University.

Have it your way.